Singapore Mainstream Preschool Teachers and the Inclusion of Children with Special Needs in their Classroom

Singapore Mainstream Preschool Teachers and the Inclusion of Children with Special Needs in their Classroom

KALAVATHI SABAPATHY

A dissertation submitted in partial fulfillment
of the requirements for the degree

of

Doctor of Education

Graduate School of Education

The University of Western Australia

December 2011

PARTRIDGE

A Penguin Random House Company

To order additional copies of this book, contact
Toll Free 800 101 2657 (Singapore)
Toll Free 1 800 81 7340 (Malaysia)
orders.singapore@partridgepublishing.com

www.partridgepublishing.com/singapore

Contents

Abstract

The aim of this study was to develop an understanding of how Singapore pre-school teachers manage children with special needs in their classes. Symbolic Interaction Theory (Blumer, 1969) provided the basis for the use of the term 'manage' to understand how people make meaning of their lives by assigning symbols in their interactions with one another. The term 'manage' as referred to by Chalmers & O'Donogue (2000), explores the strategies utilized by teachers when they have a child with special needs in their class alongside other typically developing children. These strategies could involve dealing with inappropriate behaviour as inculcating appropriate behaviour of all the students as well as ensuring that learning also takes place for all the children in the classroom.

In order to achieve the aim of the study, the participants' knowledge about children with special needs, the beliefs they hold on including these children in their classes, the strategies employed by them to carry out inclusive education and their reasons for adopting those strategies as well as the challenges faced by them in an inclusive setting were explored.

This study was a combination of a descriptive and an explanatory qualitative case study. Eight teachers from a selected preschool in Singapore were the participants of this study. Semi-structured interviews and classroom observations were utilized to gather data from the participants. This was carried out over a period of six months where participants were approached to participate in the study at regular intervals. This helped to keep track of changing perspectives during the period of study.

Miles and Huberman's (1994) framework was used for data analysis in this study. Data was displayed, reduced and conclusions drawn in the process. This resulted in recommendations being made to change various current practices in order to better manage children with special needs in mainstream schools. One such recommendation is to make training in special needs education compulsory for all teachers before they accept the offer of employment in a school which has children with special needs. This is to ensure that teachers take on their tasks with confidence and to be able to maximize the learning of all children. Another recommendation is to ensure that teachers have specific goals for each child drawn up at the beginning of the year so that they can keep track of the progress made by their students and modify their teaching strategies at regular periods such as at the end of each term. Such an educational plan should be differentiated between typically developing children and those with special needs.

It is hoped that this study might serve as a catalyst in thinking about policy changes designed to support the immersion of children with special needs into mainstream educational settings.

Chapter One:

Introduction, Background and Context

1.1 Introduction

This chapter is divided into two parts: the introduction and then the background and context part. In the first section, the aim and rationale of the study are presented, followed by an overview of the study. This includes a brief description of the study, the research questions and the data collection and methodology. Next, some general information is provided on the Singapore government's initiatives to enhance the education of children with special education needs (SEN). This is followed by a discussion of the significance of the present study. An explanation of key terms used in this study is provided. In the second section, the background and context of this study is provided. The citations in this dissertation used the form from the American Psychological Association (APA, 5th Edition).

1.1.1 Aim of research

The purpose of this study was to explore how teachers in one mainstream preschool manage children with SEN in their classes. The reasons for undertaking this research were to gain more knowledge about the strategies adopted to manage children with SEN in mainstream educational settings at preschool level and to look into the factors that may influence the implementation of these strategies. It is hoped that the results of this study might provide insights for researchers and practitioners seeking to enhance inclusive educational practices at the preschool level.

1.1.2 Rationale for the study

Over the past forty years, there has been an increased emphasis in promoting children with special needs gaining access to the common domains of life (Guralnick, 2005). It has been observed that there has recently been an international move towards including children with special needs into mainstream classrooms instead of schooling them in an isolated environment. This has raised issues and generated interest for professionals in the education field, policy-makers and researchers (Chalmers & O'Donogue, 2000). While there is a certain level of skepticism surrounding the practicality of the inclusive programme, researchers' concerns are focused on three aspects. They are concerned about the effects of the inclusion of children with special needs on typically developing children, the effects of such an inclusive setting on the development of children with special needs, and the social outcomes for these latter children when they interact with their typically developing peers (Porter, 2002).

Especially now, it is relevant to Singapore because of the government's increased focus on bridging the gap between children with SEN and typically developing children. The government of Singapore has urged the country to become an inclusive society. It believes that the progress of its society is reflected in the way disadvantaged people are treated and given support. Through the Enabling Masterplan 2012-2016 (NCSS website, 2012), it hoped to reach out to people with disabilities and help them in reaching their full potential and be included in Singapore. The aim of this initiative was to implement better integration of people with special needs into mainstream society and make it possible for them to lead independent lives. It hoped to achieve this goal through appropriate intervention services, good education and better opportunities for employment. Through these means, it envisioned people with disabilities being able to live with dignity among others.

There are mainly four guiding principles behind the Enabling Masterplan 2012-2016. They are to namely, "to take an inclusive approach towards persons with disabilities, to recognise the autonomy and independence of persons with disabilities, to take an integrated approach with the support of People, Public and Private sectors and to involve the community as a source of support and empower families to care" (NCSS website, 2012).

One specific focus of the Enabling Masterplan was to focus on early intervention and integration support for children with special needs. The intention of this focus was to establish a strong foundation in the early years of children's lives so that they would be equipped with the necessary skills to lead independent lives as adults. Through these measures it is intended that children with special needs will achieve their potential. Two of the strategies mentioned in this initiative were to provide early intervention to facilitate and enhance integration as well as to provide integration support for children with disabilities to pursue mainstream education(NCSS website, 2012).

According to education statistics in Singapore, it was observed that from 1989 to 1999, there was a sharp increase in the number of children enrolled in pre-primary educational centres (UNICEF, Division of Policy and Practice, Statistics and Monitoring Section, 2008). This meant that the educational provisions for preschool education had to expand to cater to this increasing population. Hence, more preschools are making adaptations to their programmes, one of which is the accommodation of children with special needs. More details about Singapore's preschool education system and special needs education of this age group are provided in the Background and Context section.

This study focused on preschool education because educational psychologists have emphasized the importance of imparting knowledge and values in the first six years of a child's life because these are the formative years. Garrett and Kelley (2000) found from neurological imaging studies that early education has a great impact on the physiological and structural development of a young brain. Hence, appropriate intervention in children with special needs is believed to enhance learning and increase their development potential. It is in this phase that children emulate behaviour by observing role models and form perceptions of the world.

Besides focusing of the development of children with special needs, another relevant aspect is the preparation of teachers and the provision of services for these children. Whitten and Campos (2003) conducted a study in which they observed that due to an increase in the demand for teachers in the field of special education, it was crucial to look into the level of training which these teachers undergo so that time and resources were efficiently utilized. Garret and Kelley (2000) believed that although completion of relevant teacher training through coursework and practicum is crucial, it is still insufficient to meet the necessary intervention and childhood special education needs. This is further confirmed by Hebeller, as cited in Garret and Kelley (2000), who observed that there was a shortage of manpower as well as of teachers not having the substantial knowledge and skills necessary to meet the requirements of early childhood special education.

As a result, this study chose to examine the situation at the preschool level in Singapore because this is where young children gain their initial exposure to school life before embarking on formal education in primary school.

The particular preschool in this study admits children with various special needs ranging from physical disabilities (but with mobility) to neurological developmental disabilities such as autism and ADHD. Further details about this preschool being studied are provided in the next section. Currently, although children with SEN are allowed to join the preschools, not much information is available about their admission conditions and what actual provisions are made for the inclusion of these children. Hence, my study sought to explore the real situation in a particular preschool to discover some of the strategies used by teachers to manage children with SEN alongside other typically developing children.

1.1.3 Theoretical Framework of the study

This study utilized the symbolic interaction framework to understand the phenomenon being studied. This study explored how teachers manage having a child with special needs in their classes. In this context, 'manage' is related to how people make meaning out of events they encounter in their daily interactions. (Chenitz & Swanson, 1986). In terms of its relevance to the current study, this social theory examines human interaction in response to the settings they are placed in. Likewise, this study looks into how teachers manage the situation they are in, with a child with special needs in their class. According to Blumer (1969), symbolic interaction looks at how people use symbols such as words, gestures and roles in their day-to-day interactions with one another. Through the use of these symbols, people give meaning to the world in which they live in (LaRossa & Reitzes, 1993). These meanings are derived from existing symbols through people's interactions with their environment and other people. Through understanding these symbols, we make sense of human behaviour. By having a better understanding of human behaviour we are able to develop self concept as well as knowledge of our roles in the larger social structure of society. This in turn, brings us to the larger perspective of how society influences human behaviour by its norms and values. Hence, symbolic interaction theory embodies inter-personal behaviour of human beings in society on a larger scale. As such, this theory is relevant to this study as it helps us to observe how teachers react to their situation as well as the extent to which children learn behaviour from one another. Hence, the term 'manage' suggests the different reactions of teachers who have a child with special needs in their classroom.

1.1.4 The study

This section describes the setting, the participants, the data-collection method, the research questions, the data collection and analysis, the significance of present study and the definition of key terms used in this study.

1.1.5 Setting

The preschool selected is situated in the Eastern part of Singapore. This single school was selected due to logistical considerations. Initially, three schools which admitted children with special needs into their centres were approached for their participation in this study. Due to the limited number of preschools in Singapore that allowed children with special needs to be admitted, I had some difficulty obtaining permission from the centres to carry out my study. Two of the centres which I contacted declined my request stating that they were just implementing 'inclusive education' and were wary of the negative effects of any adverse reporting that might result due to the study. Eventually, only Presbyterian Community Services preschool agreed to let me conduct the study in their preschool.

Presbyterian Community Services Singapore (PCS) is run by an Executive Committee (Ministry of Community Development, Youth & Sports (MCYS) website, 2011). Its members are elected every year by the Synod of the Presbyterian Church in Singapore. A group of professional and support staff under the leadership of the Executive Director undertakes the administration of this organization. There are four main components of the PCS operation. These are Infant Care, Childcare with Integrated Childcare Programme for children with special needs, Elder Care and Emergency Relief Fund. This study looked into the Integrated Childcare Programme (ICCP). The ICCP is an inclusive programme provided in existing Child Care Centres which allows children, aged 2-6 years, with special needs to learn alongside their regular peers. The aim of this programme is to allow the child to learn, play, socialize and grow up in a natural environment. Through this initial step, the child is prepared for entry into primary school later if he/she gains admission. The ICCP is available only in some childcare centres. In these centres, there are teachers who are specifically trained to address the educational and social needs of such children. Furthermore, the physical classroom layout also caters to children with special needs and specially designed teaching materials may be used when necessary. Currently, there are six PCS ICCP centres in Singapore funded by the Ministry of Community

Development, Youth & Sports (MCYS). Hence, PCS ICCP is managed by the policies of MCYS.

Children who successfully enrol in ICCP are admitted into classes depending on their age and ability. They take part in almost all the activities under the supervision of trained teachers. These children benefit from the programme in various ways. Children with special needs will be engaged in the same age group activities as other typically developing children. This encourages socialization among children regardless of their disability. The programme caters to the needs of children with SEN through modifications to the curriculum. In this programme, an Individual Education Plan (IEP) for each child is developed together with the parents and healthcare professionals (www.learningtrust.co.uk/special_needs, 2012). Each child's progress is monitored on a regular basis. In addition, regular parent-teacher feedback sessions are also carried out so that the programme can be improved accordingly.

According to the guidelines for admission of the ICCP, children aged 2 to 6 years with physical disability, hearing impairment, visual impairment, speech delay and developmental delay (which includes autism, dyslexia and attention deficit hyperactive disorder (ADHD)) may be admitted into the programme. In the preschool in this study, children with special needs had either autism or ADHD. More information on these conditions is provided in a subsequent sub-section.

1.1.6 Participants

Participants included 8 teachers who taught the playgroup, nursery and kindergarten 1 and 2 classes. These teachers teach mainstream children and children with special needs. In addition to teaching basic literacy skills, the teachers also attend enrichment workshops on topics such as Music and Movement, storytelling, classroom activities to enhance phonemic awareness, teacher-child interaction and awareness in Multiple Intelligences. Other than the pre-service training, the teachers also continue to attend in-service training to upgrade their skills and knowledge.

1.1.7 Data-collection method

Qualitative research was carried out mainly gathering verbal and observational data by intensive study of cases (Gall, M.D., Gall, J.P., & Borg, 2003). From the data collected, the feelings, perceptions and beliefs of the participants based on their experiences and reactions were interpreted. Over a period of 6 months, 3 semi-structured interviews and 3 observations were made with each participant. The interviews were audio-recorded and field notes were taken during observations. These were carried out with the assurance that the identities of the participants, both teachers and children, would be kept confidential. A letter signed by the researcher, describing the research, was given to each participant to sign. This was to assure the participants that this research was truly carried out for the researcher's Doctoral dissertation and that confidentiality would be respected.

Through the semi-structured interviews and observations, the researcher sought answers to the research questions stated below.

1.1.8 Research Questions

The central research question of this study was as follows:

> In a preschool in Singapore that accepts children with special needs, how do teachers manage these children in their classes in the first six months of doing so?

The study regarding the perspectives of preschool teachers on managing children with special needs was guided by the following four questions:

1. What are teachers' general views about having children with special needs in their classes?
2. What educational strategies are implemented by the teacher in the classroom to accommodate children with special needs?

3. How do teachers encourage the rest of the children in the class to accept children with special needs?

4. What kind of support do teachers expect to get from the school management committee in order to manage children with special needs?

1.1.9 Data collection and analysis

In order to find out how teachers manage children with SEN in their classes, the study was carried out at a preschool in the Eastern part of Singapore. 8 teachers were interviewed over a period of six months. In addition, observations were made in and out of the classroom context during the period of study. Data was collected and stored for analysis. Miles and Huberman's (1994) framework of data analysis was adopted to analyse the data. Memoing and coding were done to sort the information derived from the data. Conclusions were drawn at the end of the process.

1.1.10 Significance of present study

Over the past three decades, there has been a growing interest in making educational provisions for children with special needs. Yet, in most cases, there is not much evidence of the necessary actions to put into practice what has been proposed on paper in terms of policy decisions (Ainscow & Miles, 2008). Some countries still adopt general education settings to cater to children with special needs. However, the general international perspective is moving towards supporting learners' diversity (UNESCO, 2007). This is a follow-up from the belief that education is a moral right for all individuals. To date, in Singapore, there has been a dearth of research on preschool teachers handling children with SEN in mainstream classes. Some of the researchers mentioned in this dissertation are Quah et al. (2004), Poon et al. (2007) and Lian, W.B. et al. (2008). Hence, this study helps to fill part of that gap in research.

For the past decade, there has been an increase in interest in cultivating an inclusive educational environment in Singapore. Educational policy changes reflect this trend towards inclusive education. There are more provisions in admission criteria for children with SEN in educational institutions. Through collaborative efforts of preschools and parents, more children with SEN have been able to attend mainstream primary schools in recent years.

In connection with this focus on inclusive education, this study was undertaken to explore the ways in which preschool teachers manage children with SEN in their classes. Through this study, it was possible to make valuable observations about the different ways in which the teachers managed children with SEN in their classes on a daily basis.

In the next section, definitions of some key terms used in this dissertation are presented.

1.1.11 Definition of key terms used in this study

In this section, definitions of key terms are presented. Descriptions of terms such as 'special needs' and 'inclusive education' are detailed, followed by a description of the preschool education system with specific reference to special education provisions.

1.1.12 Children with special educational needs

Children with special needs are broadly defined as "children who cannot fully gain the knowledge and skills of the general curriculum because of differences in one or more of the following areas: cognitive ability, sensory functioning, creativity, physical disabilities, auditory or visual perceptions, motor skills development and functioning, social skills, attention span, hyperactivity, health conditions, culture, and language and speech abilities" (Poon-McBrayer and Lian, 2002). Based on this description, it is understandable that considerable preparation is required before schools can include children with special needs in mainstream classrooms.

According to Kanu (2008), there are twelve categories of special needs. These include:

(i)   Mental retardation
(ii)   Learning disabilities
(iii)   Emotional and behaviour disorder
(iv)   Communication disorders
(v)   Hearing loss
(vi)   Blindness and low vision
(vii)   Physical disabilities
(viii) Autism
(ix)   Severe disabilities
(x)   Multiple disabilities
(xi)   Deaf/blindness
(xii)   Gifted and talented

Children involved in this study had Autism Spectrum Disorder (ASD) and Attention Deficit Hyperactivity Disorder (ADHD). In this dissertation, children with special educational needs are referred to as children with SEN. These students have learning difficulties or disabilities which significantly affect their access to the mainstream curriculum (Frederickson & Cline, 2009). These children may need further support for various reasons like those who have motor or sensory impairments, have a learning difficulty or have emotional or social difficulties (Gibson, 2005). These are further discussed in the following section.

1.1.13 Profile of children with special needs in this study

The children with SEN in the present study have either Autism Spectrum Disorder (ASD) or Attention Deficit Hyperactivity Disorder (ADHD). Around the world, the number of children diagnosed with these two conditions is increasing at a rapid rate. These conditions are significantly related to the stress that teachers face in managing challenging behaviour usually displayed by children with these conditions (Halasz, 2002; Stiefel et al., 2008). At this point, some background information about these two conditions is presented to provide a clearer picture about the additional needs of the children with these conditions. It also serves to shed light on the challenges faced by the teachers dealing with these children in their classrooms. With better understanding of these conditions, teachers are able to trial some of the strategies recommended by researchers and educators around the world. These will be discussed in a sub-section in chapter 2.

1.1.14 Autism Spectrum Disorder (ASD)

In Singapore, approximately 216 new cases with autism are diagnosed every year (Autism Resource Centre website, 2011). The Autism Resource Centre hopes to highlight the needs of these people and to heighten awareness and understanding of autism in Singapore. The pioneers of autism research, Wing and Gould (1979), observed children in England below the age of 15 and noted that they commonly displayed 'a range of cognitive functioning, poor social interaction and communication difficulties, as well as associated developmental and learning difficulties' (Hyde et al., 2010, p. 268). From their research, it was evident that individuals with autism displayed a range of symptoms, which needed to be treated according to the severity of the affliction of each individual. While differences exist among these individuals' conditions, they generally have a triad of impairments including social impairment, language and communication impairment and rigidity of thought and behaviour (Hyde et al., 2010). These three domains of impairment are further explained by Porter (2002). Children with autism tend to have communication difficulties which may be seen as either totally non-verbal or with impaired speech. Next, these children may have little understanding of their social environment and may exhibit inappropriate behaviour. They may also have fixations on certain objects and may appear limited in their play activities. Furthermore, they may have obsessions with routines and display certain levels of rigidity. When their established structures or routines are altered, they often throw tantrums and in extreme cases, exhibit self-injurious behaviour (Porter, 2002).

1.1.15 Attention Deficit Hyperactivity Disorder (ADHD)

According to Armstrong (1996), in the late twentieth century, Attention Deficit Hyperactivity Disorder (ADHD), was the childhood complaint most frequently diagnosed and at present, is also one of the childhood conditions where research has been done on a wide scale (Carpenter & Emerald, 2009). ADHD, identified about a century ago, is usually detected between the ages of 3 and 4 (Barkley, 1998). Barkley (1998) found that there could be a neurological explanation for this condition. Some of the symptoms of ADHD are behavioural issues, emotional outbursts, difficulties in relationships, learning disabilities and some health problems (Barkley, 1998). Barkley et al. (2002) observed that people with ADHD are unable to regulate their behaviour and they are not able to think about the consequences of their behaviour. This suggests that people with ADHD tend to repeat their behaviour even if the behaviour is followed by punishment because they are not able to relate their previous experiences involving punishment to correct their behaviour.

In recent years, there has been a positive shift from ADHD being perceived as a moral defect, often linked with anti-social behaviour that cannot be treated, to understanding it as a neuro-developmental disorder which can be treated. It is one of the most common childhood disorders with a worldwide incidence of 5.29% (Polanczyk et al., 2007). In Singapore, in a survey done on 2400 children between the ages of 6 and 12, 4.9% of children had this condition (Woo et al., 2007). This is a significant figure, as this disorder affects the academic, social and occupational domains of all these children. Unfortunately, in a survey carried out on 48 general practitioner doctors (Lian et al., 2003), it was also found that the level of awareness among them about this condition was not satisfactory. Likewise, teachers were also found to have little knowledge of this condition (Lian et al., 2008).

ASD and ADHD are the two specifically different conditions of those children with SEN in this study and the strategies necessary for assisting these children are specifically different too. These are reviewed in the next chapter and revisited in subsequent chapters to explore whether and how they have been implemented and practiced in the preschool of this study.

1.1.16 Inclusive education

Internationally, there is a certain level of confusion with defining inclusion (Ainscow et al., 2000). The term 'inclusion' is itself subject to various interpretations. It is pertinent to remember that a single perspective on inclusion might not be applicable to all contexts (Dyson & Millward, 2000). Used in the context of children with special needs, inclusion suggests including children with disabilities within the mainstream education system. The basis for this stems from the belief that every child has a right to learn in an environment that allows them to maximize their potential.

An international research analysis by Ainscow et al. (2006) compiled five ways of approaching inclusion. They are: "inclusion as concerned with disability and 'special educational needs'; as a response to disciplinary exclusions; as about all groups vulnerable to exclusion; as the promotion of a school for all; and as Education for All" (Ainscow et al., 2006). Inclusive preschool education is defined as a preschool setting where preschool-age children with special needs and their typically developing peers interact and collaborate freely (Odom, 2000). Inclusive education refers to a system of education whereby disabled and non-disabled children attend school together with appropriate provisions and support necessary to facilitate learning. In education, integration means that some modifications would be made to accept learners with disabilities without much change to the existing schooling system. In comparison, inclusive education entails the re-structuring of schools so that the learning needs of all children are met (Ainscow, 2005). This involves changes in the view and subsequently the labels attached to certain groups of people. Thus, the term 'disabilities' is replaced with 'special needs'. Inclusive schooling also accepts that children can have some learning difficulties at any point during their learning journey in school, thus requiring the respective schools to constantly monitor and modify their systems in order to cater to the needs of the learners.

1.2 Background and Context

1.2.1 Introduction

In this section, information pertinent to an understanding of the situation of children with special needs in relation to preschool education in Singapore is presented. In order to set the study in context, an overview of early childhood care and education in Singapore is provided in some detail, including the policies governing the operation of these preschools or centres.

1.2.2 General information on the Singapore government's initiatives to enhance the education of children with SEN

Over the past decade, there has been greater focus on improving the educational experience of children with SEN by including them in mainstream education where possible. In line with Singapore's vision of becoming an inclusive society ("Singapore 21" website, 1999), Special Needs Officers (SNOs) were introduced to Singapore primary and secondary schools in 2005 to support children with learning disabilities so they can learn alongside their non-disabled peers in the mainstream schools. With three cohorts of SNOs already in some schools, this research aims to contribute to newly emerging discourse(s) and literature on inclusive models of educational practice, the efficacy of such a national provision and the appropriate preparation of SNOs to support the diverse abilities and needs of pupils in schools.

The Ministry of Education (MOE) of Singapore announced that it will increase its support for the education of children with SEN through higher level of placement into mainstream educational institutions, improved resources and better curriculum support from 2010 (MOE Press release, March, 2010). One of the moves to support children with SEN undergoing mainstream secondary curriculum and vocational education programmes was to increase the Edusave Pupils Fund and Edusave Grant from January 2011. Initially, the Edusave Pupils Fund for each student is $200. This was increased by $40. Likewise, the Edusave Grant for each student was raised from $50 to $90. The former fund can be used to pay for students' school fees and school enrichment programmes while the latter can be utilized for enrichment programmes or to procure more resources.

In addition, it has been recognized that children with SEN "need a firm foundation of literacy skills in order to learn, communicate effectively and live independently" (MOE Press release, 2010). In order to address this need, MOE has plans to implement Reading Mastery to all special schools gradually. This programme, called the Direct Instruction reading programme, is structured in such a way that systematic teaching of skills takes place through comprehensive lesson plans. Direct Instruction is a teaching model developed in the 1960s by Siegfried Engelman based on research done by Bereiter and Engelman (1966). This instructional model contains these salient features: scripted lesson plans, signal-based teachers, skill focused, appropriate pacing and frequent testing with corrective feedback. This programme allows a higher level of interaction between teachers and students with on-going reinforcement during learning. This programme was initially piloted in seven special schools in 2009. The success of the initiative was observed when the students showed an improvement in their reading skills after undergoing the programme. As an added benefit, it was observed that students were generally enthusiastic about reading and had better focus. While this move was good for students, teachers also felt more competent in teaching children with SEN. Based on the success of this programme, MOE has future plans to experiment with other similar programmes to show their support for improving literacy skills in children with SEN.

While the implementation of the Direct Instruction reading programme caters to the literacy skills of children with SEN, MOE is also interested in fostering better ties between children from special schools and those in mainstream schools. This increase in opportunities for interaction between the two groups of students is believed to foster better understanding of the needs of both groups. Pathlight School and Canossian School have established partnerships with mainstream schools. The goals of such an initiative are an improvement in the quality of learning experiences for children with SEN and to enhance social integration (MOE Press Release, 2010). In addition to this, mainstream schools that are in the vicinity of Special Education (SPED) schools will attempt to carry out collaborative social and learning activities through various avenues such as the Community Involvement Programme (CIP), National Education Programme and Co-curricular activities (CCAs). Furthermore, MOE will support special classes for SPED students in the mainstream schools by providing necessary resources. Some of these resources include funds for setting up special classrooms and extra manpower through Allied Educators (AEDs) who will support the teaching staff. While Pathlight School has currently established partnerships with Chong Boon Secondary and Townsville Primary, it will add on another partner, Bishan Park Secondary from 2010. This move means more interaction for its senior students with autism who will be able to have better transitioning from SPED school into mainstream post-sec institutions. MOE will also look into the existing collaborations and spread good initiatives to other schools.

While the above steps deal with SPED schools, MOE also believes in providing continuous support for students with mild special needs in mainstream schools. This is done by deploying Allied Educators (Learning and Behavioural Support) [AED (LBS)] and also by training a group of mainstream school teachers in special needs. MOE confirmed that by July 2010, all primary schools and 31 designated secondary schools would be provided with one trained AED (LBS). This would meet its 2010 target of 236 AEDs (LBS) (MOE Press Release, 2010). In future, MOE will recruit more of such support staff to deal with long term needs.

Another MOE target is to have 10 percent of all primary and secondary school teachers with training in special needs. Furthermore, MOE intends to train 10 percent more of secondary teachers, which includes Junior College and Centralised Institution teachers by 2012, so that the varied educational needs of children with SEN can be met as well as learning intervention provided where necessary. Hence, from the press release in March 2010 by MOE, it is evident that more is being planned and executed in phases to cater to the spectrum of needs of children with SEN both in special schools as well as those in mainstream schools. At this point, the measures taken by MOE to enhance its support for children with SEN at the preschool level are worth exploring. This study looked at the level of resources provided for preschool teachers to help them better manage children with SEN.

While the section above explains the extent of MOE's involvement with SEN, the next section looks into how educational organizations themselves are promoting better integration between youths with special needs and society. One such institution is Metta School, which caters to the education of students with mild intellectual disability and autism. Not long ago, it launched a structured two-year programme which would culminate in a recognized vocational certification. This programme was conducted in partnership with the Institute of Technical Education (ITE). Baking, food preparation and housekeeping were the components of this programme. Through this course, students gained work-related experience and qualifications which were advantageous when students sought employment in future. The collaborations started small and gradually moved on to larger organizations. The students were linked with the school's cleaners, a day care centre and an old folks' home. From this point, they got attached to other external organizations like McDonald's, Mr Bean, Secret Recipe, Park Avenue Suites and Royal

Plaza Hotel (www.schoolbag.sg, 2010). Working in collaboration with these organizations helps to boost youths' level of confidence in dealing with the demands of working life. Hence, these moves make it easier for children with SEN to integrate better with their mainstream peers as well as have easier transition into the working world. The examples above were cited to show the extent to which Singapore, on the whole, is moving towards a nation that is more inclusive of people with special needs.

As there is an increase in the awareness about special needs, inclusive education and enhancements in teacher training, there is a greater interest in finding strategies to manage an inclusive educational environment. Hence, research is on-going about inclusive educational possibilities in various countries including the United States.

In Singapore, there has been some level of effort through research to explore and understand inclusive education at the primary and secondary levels. However, there is a gap in inclusive educational research at the preschool level. The present study helps to fill this gap by looking at how teachers in a mainstream preschool manage children with SEN in their classes.

1.2.3 Changes in Singapore's educational approaches for children with special needs

The information provided in this section is partly based on the compilation by Quah et.al (2004). In this section, I describe how special education provision has evolved from the post-war years, changed through the post-independence years, and progressed till the 21st century. This progress is linked to the stages of Singapore's development.

1.2.4 Special Education in Singapore

During the post-war period after 1945, charitable organizations provided services for people with physical and sensory disabilities. Trafalgar Home,

Home for Crippled Children, the Red Cross Society, the Singapore Association for the Blind, the Singapore Association for the Deaf, the Canossian School for the Hearing Impaired and the School for the Deaf were some of the service providers that grew over the years to serve people with special needs. During these early years, special education functioned as a separate entity apart from the mainstream school system. As Singapore was a colony of the United Kingdom at that time, the former adopted the latter's education system which was also in place internationally at that time (Poon, Conway & Khaw, 2007).

During the post-independence years of the 1960s and the 1970s, three more schools were set up for special needs education. They were Geylang Centre, Lee Kong Chian Gardens School and Jurong Gardens School. In 1979, the Handicapped Children's Playgroup and the Christian Outreach to the Handicapped were formed to provide special needs education services. During this period there was a development of special needs services for children attending mainstream schools. In 1970, the Ministry of Health formed the Child Guidance Clinic to help children with emotional problems. This was in line with the establishment of the School Social Work and School Psychological Services at that time. Furthermore, in 1976, the School Social Work Association of Singapore was formed to counsel students and in 1978, this was named the Students Care Service. In this period, special education service provision for people with physical and sensory disabilities was extended to children with intellectual and multiple impairments. It was at this time that the Movement for the Intellectually Disabled of Singapore (MINDS) and the Association for Persons with Special Needs (APSN) were established. Concurrently, services for students with special needs attending mainstream schools were introduced.

The next two decades saw further developments of special schools such as Towner Gardens School, Yio Chu Kang Gardens School and Guillemard Gardens School. While additional services were provided for young children and adults with special needs at this time, new initiatives were beginning to emerge for very young children too. Children under three years old with special needs were able to benefit from the establishment of The Early Intervention Programme for Infants and Children (EIPIC) in 1983. Various schools such as Spastic Children's Association and the Canossian School for the Hearing Impaired began running this programme in their centres. Asian Women's Welfare Association (AWWA) started running the EIPIC programme in a special school in 1990 and Balestier Special School was formed in 1995 offering similar programmes to the Margaret Drive Special School which started operating in 1987. Students with special needs going to mainstream schools received continued support from the educational psychology service provided by the Student Care Service from 1983. In addition to this support, the TEACH ME programme was started by AWWA in 1990, to ease the integration of students with special needs into early childhood education centres. Furthermore, a team of mobile therapists were appointed to assist the needs of these children. One year later, the Dyslexia Association of Singapore was formed to serve children with dyslexia through Student Care Service. Soon after, this programme was introduced to primary school children who had dyslexia (Ministry of Education, 1995). A significant move occurred when the Learning Support Programme (LSP) was introduced to enhance the support already being given to boost the literary skills of these children (Ministry of Education, Singapore, website, 2002).

In summary, as Singapore was developing, special education also became more developed. Services which were previously provided for adults were made available to younger children. During this period, services were expanded to support students with special needs in mainstream schools. There was however a division between special education and mainstream schools, whereby both functioned as separate systems which made the possibility of inclusion rather slim.

At the beginning of the 21st century there was a significant policy shift which sought to integrate Singaporean people with special needs into mainstream society. Thus, in 2004, Prime Minister Lee Hsien Loong announced new initiatives to support students with special needs in both special and mainstream schools (Ministry of Education, Singapore, website, 2004). Prior to this announcement, Metta School was opened in

2001 followed by Grace Orchard which was established in 2002 (Poon et al., 2007). These special schools were established to assist students with mild intellectual disability and those with the Autism Spectrum Disorder (ASD). In 2006, the Singapore Autism School and the St. Andrew's Autism Centre were opened to serve students with ASD. In 2004, Pathlight School opened to educate students with high functioning ASD.

Pathlight School has three programmes to cater to the different needs of the students. One programme prepares children for primary school. Another programme allows children with ASD to undergo the mainstream curriculum in a special school. The third programme provides individualized curriculum to cater to the specific needs of the students. Pathlight has also made efforts to provide social integration by making provisions for their students to gain admission in mainstream schools and by organising collaborative activities.

With the passage of time, there has been an in increase in early intervention services provided by Rainbow Centre, AWWA Special School and Spastic Children's Association of Singapore. In addition, new services were provided by Autism Association, Autism Resource Centre, Fei Yue Community Services and the Society of Moral Charities. Similar services were provided by public hospitals like KK Women's and Children's Hospital, National University Hospital and Singapore General Hospital as well as private organisation (Ministry of Community Development, Youth, and Sports [MCYS], 2007). In 2007, the Northlight School was opened. This school is a collaborative effort by the Ministry of Education and the Institute of Technical Education. Students who have failed thrice in the Primary School Learning Examination may gain admission into this school. Here, the curriculum focuses on character, vocational education and basic literacy skills.

Besides the opening of new schools, an additional $12 million dollars was provided for recruiting qualified staff, professional development courses and curriculum development. Funds were provided not only for staffing and staff development but also for new schools and to enhance the infrastructure of schools already operating. The Ministry of Education announced in 2007, that it would open four more special schools for the hearing and visually impaired children at primary and secondary levels. Also, there was to be more special education classes in mainstream schools to supplement the services provided by Pathlight School and Canossa School for the Hearing Impaired.

There were also plans to co-locate mainstream and special schools. As for teachers, work attachments and cross-training between those teaching in mainstream and special schools was to be encouraged. Students with special needs were provided with funds to pursue certificate courses. In addition, the age span of children who could attend special schools was increased from 18 to 21 years.

From the initiatives mentioned above, it is evident that the trend has been towards providing more opportunities for children with SEN to learn skills that will help them lead a more independent lifestyle. In the next section, information on special needs support in mainstream schools will be presented.

1.2.5 What constitutes inclusion in mainstream schools?

Since the 1980s, there has been a significant change in the volume and range of services for the care of young children in Singapore. From custodial care services during the post-war period, this has evolved into a combination of 'care and education' models (AECES website, 2011). International pedagogies and philosophies have been integrated with Singapore's cultural and multi-racial values. For example, the Association for Early Childhood Educators (Singapore), has drawn up some guidelines for early childhood educators through discussion with those in the education field. Singapore endorsed the United Nations Convention on the Rights of the Child in 1995. From this comprehensive statement on children's rights, policies concerning children have been formulated and the Code of Ethics has evolved setting the standards for personnel involved in the provision of early childhood services for children up to 8 years old. Through this set of principles, ethical practice and professional growth of early educators were maintained. This has made it easier to develop competence and a sense of mission in the arena of early childhood education.

According to the above Code of Ethics, inclusive education involves planning and implementing programmes that focus on the needs, abilities and interests of children with disabilities, developmental delays and special abilities alongside typically developing peers in regular mainstream classes. These guidelines are cascaded to the various organizations through policy documents. Preschool centre principals disseminate the information to the staff through Action Plans. This in turn is taken on by respective teachers who prepare their schemes of work (SOWs). Through these documents, it can be observed how teachers manage children with SEN in their classes. The process of inclusion starts at the point of admission of these children with SEN in mainstream schools.

There is a conscious effort to reduce the number of children being placed in special schools because more of such children are chanelled to mainstream schools. This entails identifying children with mild to moderate levels of special needs and allowing placement in mainstream schools. The objectives of including children with special needs are transmitted through the processes which are in place in the various schools. Other than these, resources such as funding and staffing are re-allocated to those schools that adopt inclusion. This is crucial as inclusion entails making provisions concerning class size and facilities. To support the policy of inclusion, pre-service and in-service training are provided for teachers so that they are better prepared to take on the challenge of inclusion. Last but not least, parents have access to changes in the education policies so that they can make better-informed decisions about their children.

1.2.6 Support for children with special needs in mainstream schools

Changes in special schools policy were reflected in the initiatives developed in mainstream schools providing special needs support for their students. It was reported in The Straits Times in May 2005 (METTA website) that extra staff would be deployed to 14 schools with special needs children. These schools would get to utilize $55 million annually from 2004 to 2008. This fund would go into the training of current teachers teaching children with SEN in mainstream schools as well as the training and recruitment of Special Education Officers (SNOs). The roles of these SNOs were clearly stipulated by the Minister for Education in 2005, Mr. Tharman Shanmugaratnam. The SNOs would support children with mild to moderate dyslexia or autism to benefit from mainstream education. They would primarily provide support in the classroom with small group interventions, and small group skills training including social skills, study and organizational skills. These officers would stay with the pupils during some lessons and conduct remedial classes for them. It was mentioned that this move would have positive outcomes not only for the target group of children but for the general student population in these schools. These officers were also to deal with case management and to carry out administrative work (MOE website, 2008). This scheme was to begin on a small scale in 2005 and would be expanded till 2010 by which time all primary schools would have at least one SNO and 20 specially resourced secondary schools would have up to three SNOs to serve the needs of students with dyslexia. To serve the special needs of children with autism, 20 specially resourced primary schools and 12 specially resourced secondary schools would each be deployed with up to three SNOs. Thus, by the middle of 2009, up to 105 primary and 31 secondary schools would have SNOs working in their respective schools. In addition to the SNOs, all primary and secondary schools would have at least ten percent of teachers equipped with training to support the needs of children with (SEN). These special needs mainly include dyslexia, autism, attention deficit/hyperactivity disorder, certain learning disabilities, emotional and behavioural problems and language impairments. The SNOs were to undergo training beginning in 2005 and ending in 2010. Besides the above staff support, 59 schools would be structurally modified to allow accessibility to students with physical disabilities (Poon et al., 2007). The

Ministry of Education declared that it would be utilizing $220 million for the next four years to ensure that this policy for the transformation of inclusive education was implemented. The above-mentioned policy pronouncements were implemented according to the time frame specified.

1.2.7 Special Education (SPED) Schools

In Singapore, the educational needs of children who are medically certified to have special needs are met through the programmes run in special education (SPED) schools. These are run by Voluntary Welfare Organisations (VWOs) which receive funding from the Ministry of Education (MOE) and the National Council of Social Service (NCSS). Children with varied disabilities attend these SPED schools which run programmes that cater to the specific needs of these children. These children are deemed as not able to benefit from regular schools with mainstream curriculum. In addition to the 21 SPED schools run by VWOs, private schools such as Genesis School for Special Education and Kits4Kids Special School and foreign system schools, such as Dover Court Preparatory School, provide special education programmes (MOE website, 2011).

The aims of the programmes run by SPED schools are to develop the potential of pupils and to help them to be independent, to support themselves and to be contributing members of society (MCYS, website, 2007). In addition to receiving classroom instruction from the teachers, pupils of SPED schools gain from the involvement of psychologists, speech therapists, occupational therapists, physiotherapists and social workers. With such a team of professionals working together, it is believed that children with special needs will be trained to function optimally and be able to blend better into society.

We now turn below, to a brief profile of the relatively under-developed area of early childhood education in Singapore, the specific focus of this research study.

1.2.8 Profile of Early Childhood Education in Singapore

In Singapore, the two main early childhood services are preschools and child care centres. These are operated by individuals, communities or organisations. While the government supervises and funds the services which are not public, it does not participate in the actual running of the programmes in these services. Early childhood education involves children from age 0 to 6. At the age of 7, they start their primary school education. MCYS is the main ruling body of child care centres which cater to children from 2 months to 6 years of age. These also include preschool classes for children from 4 to 6 years old. On the other hand, preschools are run for children aged 4 to 6 only and they are supervised by MOE. According to a report in 2007, approximately, 90% of children between the ages of 4 and 6 were receiving preschool education (UNESCO Policy Brief on Early Childhood, 2007). 23% of this age group attends MCYS Child Care centres. It was also reported that 99% of children in primary 1 have at least a year of preschool education.

Kindergartens offer a 3-year preschool education for children within the age group of 3 to 6 years. This structured programme is divided into Nursery, Kindergarten 1 and Kindergarten 2. The kindergartens operate from Monday to Friday from 3 to 4 hours daily. There are usually two sessions in a day. The activities carried out aim to develop language and literacy skills, elementary mathematical concepts, basic science knowledge, social skills, creativity, problem solving skills, appreciation of aesthetics and outdoor play. In addition, children will be taught English and a Mother Tongue language.

The private sector runs kindergartens in Singapore which have to be registered with the Ministry of Education (MOE). There are foreign system kindergarten which have special programmes catered for children of expatriate parents. Child care centres also run kindergarten programmes for children aged 3 to 6. These centres are licensed by the Ministry of Community Development, Youth and Sports [MCYS] (MOE website, 2007). Some of the pre-school centres in Singapore comprise People's Action Party Community Foundation (PCF) kindergartens,

National Trade Union Congress (NTUC) childcare centres, private schools, day care centres and religious-based kindergartens.

Child care centres in Singapore do what the name suggests, caring for the child. This includes the feeding, napping, toileting, bathing and the other components of education. This differs from a kindergarten whereby children do not take a nap nor take a shower in the centre itself. They do get meal times but it is mainly like a recess break in most schools. Hence, kindergartens function more like schools while child care centres are similar to a home environment.

The desired outcomes of preschool education in Singapore are as follows: At the end of pre-school education, children will:

- Know what is right and what is wrong
- Be willing to share and take turns with others
- Be able to relate to others
- Be curious and be able to explore
- Be able to listen and speak with understanding
- Be comfortable and happy with themselves
- Have developed physical co-ordination and healthy habits
- Love their family, friends, teachers and kindergarten

(MOE website, 2011)

1.2.9 Inclusive preschool education in Singapore

In this millennium, there have been some changes in favour of inclusion in mainstream schools in Singapore (Nomanbhoy, Lim and Vasudev, 2000). The curriculum framework for pre-schools in 2003 underwent modifications which made provision to allow children with SEN to study in mainstream schools. Child care centres have been encouraged to include children with SEN into centres called Integrated Childcare Centres (ICCs). This scheme, which began in 2003 in six centres, was gradually expanded to 12 centres in 2004 (MCYS, 2004). Similarly, supportive services at pre-school level, such as TEACH ME (Therapy and Educational Assistance for Children in Mainstream Education) have been put in place. SCUBI (Supporting Children Upon Being Included), is another program which trains pre-school teachers in handling children with SEN who are admitted into mainstream schools (MOE website, 2011).

In Singapore schools, there is considerable emphasis on academic excellence as the main criterion for promotion to the next level. In a way, this can hinder the effective inclusion of children with SEN in mainstream schools because teachers are faced with the pressure to produce academic results and hence may find it difficult to include children with SEN in their classes (Chen & Tan, 2006). Inclusive education entails extra planning and execution of alternative teaching strategies, assessment modes and regular monitoring of progress made by pupils. Despite these obstacles to inclusive education in Singapore, there are a few schools which have admitted children with SEN in their pre-schools. One such pre-school is the Presbyterian Community Foundation Childcare Centre.

This study explored how PCS Child Care Centre managed having children with SEN in its classes. It did this through interviews with the teachers and through observation sessions carried out during the six month course of this research period. Through these sessions, teachers who were dealing with children in mainstream education settings were given a platform to voice their thoughts and feelings about their experiences. From these interviews, it was possible to gain an insight into how teachers manage children with SEN in their classrooms.

1.2.10 Preschool teacher training and qualifications

The quality of preschool provision depends greatly on the teachers' involvement and their level of competency. Based on the efforts taken to train teachers to equip them with the necessary skills and to continually upgrade their current knowledge of pedagogies and management skills, opportunities will be available for preschool education in Singapore to leverage itself to be on par or even exceed international practices. Different levels of training are provided for teachers so that they in turn can create a conducive learning environment for preschoolers, impart social skills and values and prepare students to face the real world.

The Pre-school Qualification Accreditation Committee (PQAC) was created in 2001 to monitor the training of preschool teachers who are teaching in Kindergarten and child care centres (MOE website). This effort was supported by Ministry of Education (MOE) and Ministry of Community Development, Youth and Sports (MCYS) (refer to diagram below).

Composition of the PQAC

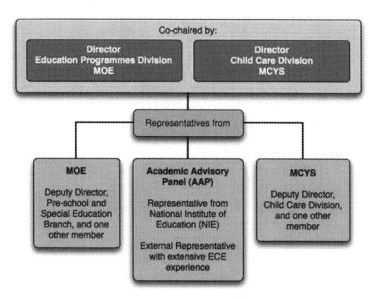

According to the changes made to the requirements of preschool teachers in Singapore, existing teachers (registered as at 31 December 2008) must have 'O' level English credit and Diploma in Preschool Education-Teaching (DPE-T) to teach Kindergarten 1 and 2 (K1 and 2). All new teachers (registered on or after 1 January 2009) must have 'O' level English credit and Diploma in Preschool Education-Teaching (DPE-T) to teach K1 and 2. 75% of all teachers in each centre must meet the requirement to teach K1 and 2. Besides these requirements, there is a training route framework called the Pre-School Education (PSE) introduced by MOE and MCYS. This would allow teachers to take up Certificate and Diploma courses according to the specified academic entry points. For those who have polytechnic diplomas or degrees from other disciplines, there is the Specialist Diploma in Pre-school Education. This programme combines the teaching and leadership aspects of both DPE-T and the Diploma in Preschool Education-Leadership (DPE-L). The information presented so far can be viewed in the diagram given below. So, these changes reflect the overall effort to improve the standard of preschool education by giving opportunities for current teachers to upgrade themselves as well as ensuring that the new teachers who enter the profession adhere to the higher entry requirements.

Pre-school Teacher Training Route (taken from MOE website: www. moe.gov.sg)

Training Pathways from 1 Jan 2009 - 31 Dec 2012

To Note:
Route A → D → E is open only to existing teachers registered with MOE / MCYS and will not be available after 31 Dec 2012.

MOE - MCYS Framework

I) Post-Graduate Studies in Early Childhood Care & Education

H) Bachelor Degrees in Early Childhood Care & Education (local / overseas)

F) Diploma in Early Childhood Care & Education - Leadership (DECCE-L)

G) Specialist Diploma in Early Childhood Care & Education (SDECCE)

E) Diploma in Early Childhood Care & Education - Teaching (DECCE-T)

D) Certificate in Early Childhood Care & Education (CECCE)

B) GCE 'O' Level credits in 5 different subjects, including a credit* in EL1 or MT.

C) University Degree / Polytechnic Diploma including a credit* in EL1 at GCE 'O' Level.

A) GCE 'O' Level credits in 3 different subjects, including EL1 or MT

* The sector teacher requirement in B4 in EL1 / MT; from 1 Jan 2009, new teachers must meet this language requirement and obtain a DPE-T/DECCE-T to be granted teacher certification status.

1.2.11 Conclusion

In this chapter, two sections were presented: the first one stated the aim and rationale of the study and gave a broad account of the study. The second one provided relevant information on the background and context of special needs education in Singapore. This was further subdivided into special education in Singapore and what constitutes inclusion in mainstream schools in the local context. The nature of support available for children with SEN in mainstream schools was then discussed, followed by preschool education and inclusive preschool education in Singapore.

The next chapter reviews the literature which explores empirical studies on how teachers manage children with SEN in mainstream classes, particularly at preschool level.

Chapter Two:

Literature Review

2.1 Introduction

This chapter reviews empirical studies related to how mainstream teachers manage children with SEN in their classroom. The discussion justifies the research questions and is organized according to these 4 research questions in order to better explain the situation being studied.

The guiding questions of this study are as follows:

1. What are teachers' general views about having children with special needs in their classes?
2. What educational strategies are implemented by the teacher in the classroom to accommodate children with special needs?
3. How do teachers encourage the rest of the children in the class to accept children with special needs?
4. What kind of support do teachers expect to get from the school management committee in order to manage children with special needs?

The literature review was organized generally according to these guiding questions so that each section could focus on key related aspects of how mainstream teachers manage children with SEN in their classroom. The 4 main focuses are:

1. teachers' general beliefs about teaching children with SEN;

2. strategies implemented in the classroom;
3. acceptance of children with SEN by typically developing children and,
4. support for teachers who need to manage children with SEN.

The studies which are mentioned in this chapter were fundamental to locating the present study. Cross references have been made among the studies to bring out their relevance to the present study.

Firstly, it would be useful to look at the definition of inclusion. Researchers generally agree that there cannot be a definition of inclusion that encompasses the various domains of inclusion accurately (Dyson & Millward, 2000). Generally, it refers to integrating children of mixed abilities (Sakarneh, 2008)

O'Brien (2001) firmly believes in allowing children with SEN to be in an inclusive educational setting and not segregated in any way. He cautions that this should not be a mere admission provision but a situation that accepts them morally and physically in a regular classroom and providing them with the necessary educational needs. In a study conducted by Banerji and Dailey (1995), students with SEN showed academic progress as well as improvement in self-esteem and motivation. Furthermore, Vaughn et al. (1996) found from their studies that an increase in the number of mutual friendships cultivated by being in an inclusive environment. In an inclusive setting, teachers are faced with various considerations such as organizational matters, management decisions such as teacher student ratio and staff working hours, implementing suitable teaching strategies as well as managing the behaviour of the children. Hence, it is crucial that the teachers facing an inclusive classroom setting have the necessary skills that would ensure an optimal learning experience for the children.

Ainscow et al. (2000) refer to five ways of approaching inclusion. The first one concerns disability and special educational needs. One critique of this perspective is that it further segregates children with additional needs leading to further marginalization (Corbett, 2001). Instead of these identifying labels, Ainscow et al. (2006) suggest looking into the 'barriers of learning and participation' and 'resources to support learning and participation', by shifting the focus from classifying children with disabilities to removing obstacles that hinder the education of children with SEN.

While experts and professionals in the education field are aware of the challenges facing inclusive education, the general trend is towards making effective educational provisions for all children within mainstream settings. This was prompted by the Salamanca Statement in 1994, which advocates inclusion on the basis of human rights (UNESCO, 1994). Dyson and Millward (2000) called this shift from special education provision for children with SEN to equal opportunities for all aqes, the 'organisational paradigm' of inclusive education. Booth and Ainscow (2002) re-iterate this shift in focus as moving away from looking at the qualities of the children and families for their educational failure to re-looking at the barriers to the involvement and learning of children within the general educational systems (Booth & Ainscow, 2002). Some of the barriers highlighted by these researchers are specifically inadequate resources or professional involvement, unsuitable curricula and perceptions. These issues have formed the basis of the research questions of the current study.

Ainscow and Miles (2008) argue that teachers play a vital role in developing an effective inclusive educational setting. In fact, their perceptions directly have an impact on the structure and process of an inclusive educational system. It is important to investigate how teachers manage children with SEN together with other typically developing children in a mainstream setting because of its impact on teachers' decisions to stay in the profession or to look for alternative careers. Attrition studies done in the United States show that approximately 30% of new teachers quit teaching within the initial five years of joining the service (Darling-Hammond, 2003; Wilkins-Canter et al., 2000). When new teachers leave the teaching profession prematurely, it creates a situation where there is little room for expertise to grow and, consequently, in the long run, this diminishes the general productivity in the education field. From research it is evident that one of the new teacher's concerns is classroom management (Ladson-Billings, 1994;

Renard, 2003). Therefore, it is vital to observe what actually happens in the classroom environment where there are children with different abilities and needs and explore how different teachers manage their students. Hence, the first research question looks into the beliefs of teachers on having children with SEN in their classes.

Next, I will present some findings from the literature about the positive and negative features of inclusive education.

2.2 General beliefs about teaching children with special needs in mainstream classes

Booth and Ainscow (2000) believe that all students and staff should be valued equally. This applies to students being treated the same without prejudice regarding their special needs. In addition, teachers should also feel that they are viewed the same as other teachers who are dealing with typically developing children. Only when society's general perceptions of children with SEN and the teachers who teach them change for the better, will the teachers themselves feel good about dealing with children with SEN. Booth and Ainscow (2000) are of the opinion that it would be beneficial if differences between students are looked upon as resources to enhance learning instead of as problems to deal with. This is essential so that teachers will not be stressed with handling children with SEN. Instead, their minds would be open to more learning and teaching opportunities. Furthermore, it is crucial for teachers to believe in the rights of children with SEN to education (Booth & Ainscow, 2000). Only then would teachers see the purpose of all the effort that has to be put into educating these children.

2.2.1 Positive responses to inclusion

Over the past two decades there has been a positive trend whereby more people are receptive to this idea. It has been found through literature reviews that children with special needs who are educated in inclusive settings perform as well as those in special schools (Lamorey & Bricker, 1993; Buysse, Goldman & Skinner, 2002). Mastropieri et al. (2004) believe that an inclusive education has positive effects on social relationships, communication, friendship, self-esteem and confidence through a reduction of labelling. Furthermore, there are studies that found that there is better performance when children with special needs receive education in an inclusive environment (Hundert et al., 1998). Researchers have observed that children with special needs who study in an inclusive setting showed positive behaviour as they take part in classroom activities together with other typically developing children (Guralnik et al., 2005).

In stressing the importance of a positive belief system of teachers in order to effectively deliver a particular lesson, Hargreaves (2009) reinforces the notion that pedagogical decisions are based on teachers' own experiences and assumptions. Villa et al. (1996) conducted a study which revealed positive feelings amongst teachers regarding having children with SEN in mainstream classrooms. It is significant that the teachers showed more commitment after they had gained a substantial level of experience in implementing inclusion. Likewise, from Sparling's (2002) study, it is evident that while teachers generally had positive perceptions of having children with SEN in their classes, insufficient knowledge about children with special needs and insufficient training in managing these children in mainstream educational settings have been the main concerns for them. Thus, from research, it can be seen that teachers on the whole have positive feelings about having children with special needs in their mainstream classes although certain concerns were present.

One possible reason for the teachers' positive mindset could be their awareness about inclusive education. Yet, their lack of technical knowledge of managing these children with special needs alongside their typically developing peers can affect their confidence level in handing such a class of students. With knowledge available to teachers about the situation they are in, they are able to confidently face the situation in their classes (Kristensen, 2002). LeRoy and Simpson (1996) investigated the effect of inclusion by conducting a longitudinal study in Michigan. They found that when teachers have better experience in dealing with children with SEN, they displayed more confidence in dealing with them.

In the United Kingdom, a study was conducted to observe the extent to which pedagogical decisions are based on fixed beliefs about the ability of students (Ainscow et al., 2006). The researchers began the study on the assumption that limitations to children's learning are evident when the pedagogical decisions are based on the abilities of the children. The definition of 'ability' was not clarified here and the teachers were left to their own interpretation of the term. It was observed that these teachers believed that the capability of the learners is not fixed but can change over time. Hence, with this mind-set, the teachers looked out for gaps between the students' potential and what was happening in their classrooms. Thus, making superficial changes to the lesson delivery would not make any significant change in the learning of the children as the deep-rooted beliefs of the teachers are still embedded in the teachers. Next, some unfavourable views on inclusion are presented.

2.2.2 Negative responses to inclusion

In spite of the numerous benefits of inclusive education cited from research, not everyone in the field of education is convinced to adopt inclusion and some even have an aversion to the whole idea (Freire & Cesar, 2002). In fact, there are some educationists who advocate a separate system for disabled people because they strongly believe in providing exclusive care in a system that provides specialized services (Freire & Cesar, 2002). Kristensen et al. (2006) refers to the situation in Uganda whereby special provisions made for children with special needs, in terms of professional involvement, resources and assistance were more useful to the target group as this group did not have sufficient support in mainstream educational settings. Although there have been positive reviews about inclusive education, in analyzing seventeen Education

For All (EFA) plans from the South and South-East Asia region, Ahuja (2005) found that inclusive education was not even featured in the discussion. In fact, she found that special schooling provisions and special accommodation arrangements were recommended for children with special educational needs. According the report by United Nations (2005), such modes of institutionalization do have negative effects. Although a study of countries involved in the Fast Track Initiative of EFA found that there were plans to address inclusive education (World Vision, 2007), these policies and provisions for children with special needs have been at a superficial level and have not been concretely implemented.

Cook (2001) investigated the connection between teachers' attitudes towards children with SEN in their classes and the severity of the special needs. He conducted a study on 70 teachers who manage children with SEN in mainstream classes and found that the teachers' attitudes varied according to the severity and obviousness of the disability. One consequence of such an attitude is there is a risk of students not receiving necessary educational interventions. At the end of the study, some recommendations for improving teachers' attitudes towards children with SEN with hidden and obvious disabilities were presented. One of the suggestions is for teachers to continuously upgrading their knowledge and skills through training. Another way is to share their perceptions with a knowledgeable special education teacher who would be able to give a clearer picture of the various disabilities so that any biases that the teachers may have can be eradicated. When the teachers' stereotyping views are altered, then it would be feasible to put into actual teaching practice better teaching strategies that would enhance the learning of children with SEN (Cook, 2001). Overall, it would be a good idea to be more aware of the perceptions of teachers as they influence the decisions made about teaching students.

Coates (1989) studied the perceptions of mainstream teachers in Iowa on having children with SEN in mainstream classes and found that they did not object to the "pullout" programmes. This refers to a situation in which if a child with SEN cannot fit into the current system of a school, his or her parents can withdraw him or her and admit him or her in a more suitable school. In addition, they were not in favour of inclusion. Semmel et al. (1991) studied 381 primary school teachers of both mainstream schools and special schools and found that they did not object to a special education programme that allowed "pullout" options to parents of children with SEN. Wilmore (1995) noted that some teachers felt that by having children with SEN in their classes, they would be spending more time baby-sitting them at the expense of spending constructive time with the rest of the class. Vaughn et al. (1996) investigated the perceptions of mainstream and special educators regarding inclusive education and found that most of them had rather negative views about inclusion and felt that those in authority did not have an understanding of the reality of the inclusive education system in schools. According to them, size of class, having adequate resources, assurance of benefit to students and sufficient preparation of teachers were some of the factors that would ensure successful inclusion. It is significant to note that these teachers who had negative opinions regarding inclusion, at the point of research, were not teaching in an inclusive setting. On the other hand, those who had taught in an inclusive setting before had different viewpoints.

From the examples cited above, it is evident that though teachers may initially have some negative attitudes towards teaching children with SEN, these may change over time after they have gained more experience in implementing various strategies.

2.3 Strategies recommended and / or implemented to accommodate children with special needs in mainstream classes

Firstly, I will present key strategies recommended by researchers to cater to the needs of the two specific kinds of special needs that the children of the current study have, that is, Autism and ADHD. After that, I will present other strategies recommended for an inclusive educational environment.

2.3.1 Suggested strategies for children with Autism

Picture Exchange Communication System (PECS)

One strategy useful to develop communication in children with speech delay is the picture exchange communication system (PECS), (Bondy & Frost, 2001). This system primarily involves the use of pictures to assist in the children's communication. At the initial stage, the child is given a few pictures of the child's favourite item such as a toy of food. If the child requests one of the items, he hands over the corresponding picture to the partner dealing with him in this situation. Then, that person gives the child the required item. This kind of exchange is believed to encourage communication. Besides being a mode of getting things, PECS can also be used to describe the environment. For example, when a child sees a cat, he gives a picture of a cat to his communicating partner. Gradually, when the child understands the effectiveness of this tool, it is hoped that in the long run, he will start to use natural speech (Charlop-Christy et al., 2002). What makes PECS effective is the immediate reward that acts as the direct reinforcement. Without the need for speech, the child is able to satisfy his inner craving with external gratification. With proper training and guidance in PECS, is believed that this system can help children with autism in their social interactions. Empirical research studies have proven the usefulness of PECS (Tien, 2008). In a study involving 18 preschool children who had speech delay, it was found that they could use PECS for communication on a daily basis in school. In addition, about half of these children became verbal within one year (Schwartz, et al., 1998). On the whole, there is much evidence from various studies that suggest that when PECS is taught to children before the age of six, it is effective as a tool to develop natural communication (Mirenda, 2008 & Tien, 2008). As a further support for the use of PECS, there is also evidence from research that children with autism who use PECS develop speech faster than those who do not (Bondy, 2001; Bondy & Frost, 2001).

Applied Behaviour Analysis (ABA)

Another strategy recommended by experts is the Applied Behaviour Analysis (ABA) approach which teaches social, motor and reasoning skills and verbal behaviours (Harris & Delmolino, 2002). Experts believe that ABA is specifically effective for children with autism who may not pick up appropriate behaviours unlike their peers. The way ABA works is by rewarding appropriate behaviour and removing triggers of inappropriate behaviours by themselves (Simpson, 2001). The triggers are replaced with new reinforcers to teach the child an alternative behaviour (Jensen & Sinclair, 2002). The logic behind implementing this strategy is the experts' belief that children who have autism have little possibility of learning appropriate behaviour from their natural environment they function in on a daily basis (Lovaas, 1987). Hence, the ABA strategy assists in bridging this gap through systematic, manageable instructions and reinforcement that is given consistently. On the whole, with proper use of the ABA approach, it is believed that children with autism can be more independent and socially functional (Lovaas, 1987). Further emphasizing the effectiveness of this approach are the findings through research that when children with autism receive early intervention at the preschool level, the outcome is positive. The reason behind this is the fact that when children are at the preschool age, they go through crucial brain development which can be impacted by training (Jensen & Sinclair, 2002; Rosenwasser & Axelrod, 2001). There is evidence from research to show that ABA is an effective strategy to be used in children with Autism (Simpson, 2001a). The U.S. Surgeon General vouches that three decades of research has indicated the effectiveness of the ABA approach when as an early intervention tool for children with autism (U.S. Department of Health and Human Services, 1999). This research further points that when children receive ABA therapy it helps them to be in inclusive classes (Howard et al., (2005); Cohen et al. (2006)). Generally, there has been an increase in the use of the ABA therapy and there has been more support for its use worldwide (Bloh & Axelrod, 2009). In fact, it was observed in a study that ABA therapy was more effective compared to other intervention plans for children with autism. Specifically, when ABA therapy is used with high-intensity, it is very effective during the preschool years (Ospina et al., 2008).

2.3.2 Suggested strategies for children with ADHD Behavioural management

Research has shown that behavioural management is highly recommended as a strategy to aid the learning of children with ADHD. This comprises practical help with school work completion, educating children on appropriate social behaviour and also ways to monitor their own behaviours (Fung & Lee, 2009). The extent to which a child performs in adulthood is dependent on the effective parenting skills of the child's parents, the child's socializing skills with his or her peers and the child's level of success in school (Hinshaw, 2002). Therefore, as recommended by researchers, intervention treatments should begin at the earliest possible time once the child has been diagnosed with the condition (Webster-Stratton, et al., 2001; August, et al., 2001). Behaviour modification is one of the strategies recommended by researchers in the area of ADHD. This comprises mainly three segments. They are, the things that trigger certain behaviours, the actual behaviour of the child and the effects of that behaviour. In behaviour modification programmes, adults make changes to the triggers, like the instructions given to the child, and the consequences of the child's behaviour, such as the adults' reaction to the compliance or disobedience of the child. Through consistently modifying these, it is hoped to have an impact on the child's behaviour over time (American Academy of Pediatrics, 2001). Researchers recommend incorporating four points into behaviour modification. They are to begin with achievable goals, being consistent, putting in effort on a long-term and allowing time for the child to learn new skills. Hence, teachers should also keep these recommendations in mind in order to effectively assist children with ADHD (American Academy of Pediatrics, 2001).

Research has shown that it is important that children with ADHD receive interventions to develop their social skills as these children usually have difficulties in establishing social relationships (Bagwell et al., 2001). Thus, in addition to the strategies recommended so far, experts suggest that social skills should be taught in a systematic way (Webster-Stratton, 2001). Children with ADHD, should also be educated on the ways to solve social problems (Houk et al., 2002) and other behavioural skills. On the whole, there should be efforts to reduce inappropriate behaviours (Walker et al., 1995) and to foster a deep bond with friends.

Booth and Ainscow (2000) recommend that while planning lessons, teachers should be mindful of "reducing barriers to learning and participation for all students, not only those without impairments or those who are categorized as having SEN children". This means that the provisions made for learning of all students collectively so that regardless of special needs, every student can benefit from the changes made. Another point mentioned by Booth and Ainscow (2000) is that teachers could learn from the efforts made to remove obstacles to facilitate the inclusion of certain groups of students to make changes to the general student population. This means that whenever certain educational strategies are implemented, teachers could learn from their efforts in making implementation possible.

A few strategies have been utilized in situations where children with SEN are present in an educational setting alongside typically developing peers. From research findings available from the Early Childhood Research Institute on Inclusion (2000), it was suggested that children with special needs in an inclusive educational setting be given specialized instruction in order for the inclusive programme to be effective at the preschool level. While keeping such instruction as uniform as possible, teachers could merge it with the other activities carried out in the classroom.

Lewis et al. (1998) recommend that it is essential to lay down ground rules, specify inappropriate behaviour and to inculcate acceptable social behaviour. Furthermore, the teacher's role extends itself to "moving around, scanning, interacting with the students, reinforcing displays of targeted social skills". This entails active participation on the part of the teachers and specifies their role clearly as being the facilitators to encourage appropriate social behaviour through "reminders, prompts and rehearsals prior to problematic times or settings" (Lewis et al., 2000: 111). Through observation of real classroom settings, this practice appeared to "effectively reduce rates of problem behaviour across the student body" (Lewis et al., 2000: 111). Thus, it is essential for teachers to be clearly aware or their role in managing their students.

Generally, there are three suggested instruction modes: whole-class instruction, cooperative learning and the individual student system. In whole-class instruction, students are encouraged to participate in class activities. This is usually carried out by first the teacher demonstrating a skill, after which the students imitate that skill through "guided and independent practice" (Stright & Supplee, 2002, p.12). While this may be a common practice in schools, Stright and Supplee (2002), concluded that students were less inclined to "monitor their own progress or to seek help" (Stright & Supplee, 2002, p.12). One of the reasons for this could be the students' perception of teacher-directed instruction as "an inactive time in the classroom". On the other hand, this type of teaching method has its merits too. Nelson et al. (1996) observed students who had Emotional-Behavioural Disorders (EBD) and found that these students' performance got better during teacher-directed instruction. They were able to follow instructions and were on task with lesser displays of disruptive behaviour.

Next, in cooperative learning, students work in teams of not more than four to complete an assigned task. Studies have shown that this type of learning encourages team work and cooperation among students and in the process students learn healthy ways to resolve conflict and share their views productively (Mulryan, 1995). From his study, Mulryan (1995) concluded that "students' engagement was much greater in the small-group than in the whole-class setting" (Mulryan, 1995). Cooperative learning allows the teacher the time and space to walk around the class to supervise and guide students as they work at their own pace in groups.

Another mode of instruction allows students to work independently with minimal assistance. According to Walker et al. (1996), when students need to have specialized learning due to behaviour issues or other reasons which inhibit the student's learning in other classroom arrangements, "the individual system provides established policies and procedures for responding to students who present the most severe forms of behaviour" (Walker et al., 1996:198). Hence, the teacher has the liberty to exercise discretion in choosing among the three types of instruction depending on the objectives, needs and the dynamics of the class. Whatever the mode of instruction the teacher uses, Doyle (1986) suggests four principles for the classroom instruction to be effective. They are to clearly stipulate expected behaviors, to ensure that students have the skills to display appropriate behaviour, to continually monitor the progress of an implementation, and to create and maintain a condusive environment for the above three to take place.

It has been emphasized by Noonan and McCormick (1993) that using instructional strategies that maintain the natural flow of classroom activities, brings about optimal benefits to both children with SEN as well as those typically developing children. They suggest that it would be good if instructional interactions occur in the natural environment. During the observations made during the data-collection sessions, this was one point that was noted. It was also suggested that interactions are kept brief and spaced over a period of time. This too was noted during my informal observation sessions which will be discussed later.

Additionally, Noonan and McCormick stated that it is good if interactions are child-initiated using natural consequences like those familiar to the child. Overall, observations were made to see if these features were present in the preschool that was studied. Generally, scaffolding is recommended by Noonan and McCormick (1993) as it provides necessary support for the children through the use of various kinds of prompts.

When it comes to teaching interdependence, Noonan and McCormick (1993) stress the need to gradually allow children to become more independent as they get older. At the preschool level, students are generally encouraged to be independent during classroom routines (Hains et al., 1989). This is the reason why most preschools plan activities that provide opportunities for independent behaviour.

According to Pressley and McCormick (1995), children with SEN benefit most from one-to-one contact with the teacher. This creates opportunities for students to grow academically and intellectually as it creates an environment which allows students to explore concepts. The teachers, too, are able to work closely with students to guide them according to their specific needs. Although research supports individual attention for children with SEN, it is generally not practical to be implemented in actual classroom settings over a long period because of staff-student ratio limitations. Alternatively, as students do their work individually, the teacher should attend to those children who need that extra prompting or checking (Pressley & McCormick, 1995). In addition, the teacher could spend time after school hours with those children who need that extra attention if the situation warrants it. During these one-on-one tutoring moments, the teacher can gain a better understanding of the special needs of the children concerned. From this understanding, perhaps future lessons can be modified to enhance the level of absorption of the concepts taught.

However, Pressley and McCormick (1995) warn of the risk of attending to the needs of the small groups of students at the expense of leaving advanced learners bored. It was suggested that at this juncture, those who can learn fast can be assigned more challenging tasks or be partnered with a slower student for peer tutoring duties. However, Pressley and McCormick (1995) caution that some students can become over-reliant on teachers due to their lack of confidence and inability to function on their own. Over time, this situation may lead to these children monopolizing the time of the teacher. Pressley and McCormick (1995) suggest that in such a situation, the teacher can give these children general guidance and meet them separately after school hours to tend to their special queries. One time-saving strategy is to combine those who have similar questions into a group and address their concerns collectively. Another strategy is to get those who are more competent and more confident to take on the role of mentors to guide those who need extra help with their work (Pressley & McCormick, 1995).

According to Sparling (2002), the teacher in the classroom can model positive behaviour for the students to emulate. Also, he suggested that teachers can hold light-hearted conversations with specific groups of students in order to ease the initial discomfort the students may face in each other's company. Using these informal strategies, teachers can assist in making it easier to allow children with SEN to merge into the mainstream classroom.

Several strategies are recommended by Duhaney (2004) in terms of managing children with SEN in mainstream educational settings. He states that it is essential for teachers to be aware of the structural layout of their classrooms and to note if the current arrangement is conducive for the learning of all students including those with SEN. If it is not optimal, then the teacher could perhaps make some changes and observe the consequences for a while before making further changes over time. Teachers are advised to monitor their classroom procedures carefully and observe if their instructions are effective in minimizing disruptions to the students' learning. With minimal disturbances to routines, students will be able to focus on their learning and be more settled in their behaviour too (Duhaney, 2004). Another strategy is for teachers to review the content of the lessons taught and to see if certain areas can be modified so that they cater to the interests of the students. In this way, students will be more engaged and are more likely to find the whole process of learning meaningful. Lastly, Duhaney (2004), suggests that teachers have direct communication with the students on an individual basis in order to understand the specific needs of the students concerned so that specific behaviour modification techniques can be implemented.

One strategy recommended by Korpan, et al. (1997) is to explore alternative learning environments for students. Their research revealed that exposure to learning environments outside of the school can provide a rich source of motivation for children with SEN. This is the reason why schools conduct learning journeys and excursions for students. From these trips, students get to see different perspectives because the learning environment is altered and so is the input from the lesson delivered. By exposing students to various possibilities beyond the school boundaries, teachers can possibly unleash hidden talents which can be more evident in informal settings. While learning out of the school compound seems to be a common practice for many schools at present, its special benefit to students with SEN should not be underestimated.

In the preschool that participated in this study, I looked into the activities to see if some of the strategies mentioned above, were put into practice. In chapter 4, there will be an examination of how some of these strategies were implemented to manage children with SEN in mainstream classes.

2.4 Acceptance of children with special needs by typically developing children

While examining the attitudes and mindsets of teachers is crucial, it is also relevant to observe the efforts made to encourage acceptance of children with SEN by other typically developing children.

From the literature available on preschool inclusion, it has been found that early childhood interaction with children with SEN has long-term effects on the perceptions of individuals when they become adults. Diamond, Hestenes, Carpenter & Innes (1997) found from their research that "typically developing children's knowledge of disabilities, their overall acceptance of individuals without disabilities, and their participation in an inclusive class contributed significantly and independently to their acceptance of children with disabilities" (Diamond et al., 1997, p. 520). In support of this, there has been an overview study done which focused on crucial behavioural and social impact on young children in inclusive educational settings (Brown, Odom, Shouming Li & Zercher, 1999).

Literature review of inclusive preschool education suggests the following. Firstly, it creates opportunities for students to learn appropriate behaviour through modelling and imitation, in addition to providing a platform to rehearse learnt behaviour with other students (Diamond et al., 1997). Usually, young children internalize appropriate social skills and routines in a structured environment such as the preschool. They observe their teacher's and peers' behaviour and tend to demonstrate what they have learned in their own behaviour. It was also found that as young children's peer interactions become more frequent at the level of preschool, their peers increasingly become their role models. This imitation of peers serves to encourage appropriate social behaviours amongst young children. This notion is also supported by Bricker (2000) who observed that when typically developing children are placed in an environment consisting of children with SEN, the children were able to learn new skills and information by observing "relevant and appropriate" models who were displaying acceptable social behaviour.

Secondly, this early exposure to children with SEN can cause a positive change in the mindsets of typically developing children so that there will be more of them opting for their classmates with SEN as their partners (Nabors, 1997a). It can be observed from research that children are moulded through social interaction. Hence, it is important to manage the social dynamics of preschools because this is where young children develop a sense of who they are and are more aware of their partnering preferences (Erwin, Alimaras & Price, 1999). This is the earliest stage where group dynamics are subtly evident during work and play time. It has also been found in research that children who start their preschool education without much social skill often encounter behavioural and academic problems which they then carry over to their secondary school and future life as well (Buysse, Goldman & Skinner, 2002). This suggests that if children do not have a strong foundation in basic life skills at a young age, it would be rather challenging to adapt and learn these skills as they get older. In support of this finding, Nabors (1997a) found that when typically developing children and those with SEN interact in a common setting, they are able to learn social skills better than if they were to be exposed to them in an exclusive setting. Furthermore, it has been found through research that typically developing children who take part in activities with children with special needs in inclusive settings showed a positive attitude towards children with special needs (Peck, Carlson, & Helmsetter, 1992). Not only that, it also enhances their understanding of certain disabilities (Diamond et al., 1997).

While there are positive outcomes in the acceptance of children with special needs through an inclusive education setting, there are some negative realities too. Based on a review from 1996, children with special needs tend to socialize less with their typically developing peers in inclusive educational environments (Guralnick et al. 2005) than in special school environments. This could stem from various factors such as the difficulties faced by children with special needs in the domains of social, emotional, communication, motor, and behavioural development as well as academic learning (Alper & Ryndak, 1992).

Guralnick (1999) also suggests that the effectiveness of inclusive programmes in encouraging typically developing children to accept those with special needs can only be effective if parents are involved in the school's efforts. Odom (2000) notes with caution that the criterion for socially acceptable behaviour could vary among individuals with SEN depending on the nature of the disability they have. Thus, educators should be mindful of setting realistic goals for them. This could have long-term benefits in preparing young children for their future primary and secondary school life subsequently whereby they would probably co-exist with children with SEN (Odom, 2001; Bricker, 2000). The experiences which these children have in their preschool years will inevitably affect the way they view children with SEN later on in their lives. In fact, when typically developing children interact with children with SEN at a young age, it develops the former's sensitivity towards the latter and this consequently has an impact on the children's general understanding and acceptance of differences of individuals (Diamond et al., 1997).

A qualitative study was carried out by Sparling (2002) at a high school in the United States of America (US) to investigate the factors that affect the extent to which students accepted peers with SEN. Some of the factors mentioned were the type of disability, social and cultural impact, teacher perceptions and peer pressure. It was found in Sparling's (2002) study that there were five main factors that affected the level of acceptance of peers with SEN among typically developing students. Firstly, the students felt unsure about dealing with those with SEN due to insufficient information about special needs. Secondly, peer pressure inhibited students from mingling freely with those with disabilities. Thirdly, the school's focus was on academic achievement which did not allow the modifications to be made to the current school culture to facilitate the co-schooling of those with SEN. Fourthly, the presence of varying disabilities hindered conventional communication modes and at times resulted in awkward interactions. Lastly, teacher attitude which was closely related to the way students viewed those with disabilities and consequently affected the level of acceptance of those with SEN was a significant factor that had an impact on the level of acceptance of students with SEN.

In Sparling's (2002) study, 82% of typically developing students revealed that they would be forthcoming in rendering assistance to students with SEN if they were requested to do so. It is significant that 60% mentioned that they would socialize more with those with SEN if they were taught how to interact with those with SEN. 68% of those who participated in this study shared that those with intellectual and physical special needs would blend in with the rest better if those without special needs had better knowledge about the kinds of special needs they have. All these findings emphasise the point that having sufficient knowledge about disabilities is a key determinant affecting the acceptance by others of children with SEN into mainstream educational settings.

Given the changing educational landscape of education in Singapore, which is gradually making more provisions for children with SEN to be schooled together with their typically developing peers, it is, arguably, crucial to introduce an inclusive academic setting to young children at the initial stage of their education at the preschool level so that when they move up to primary and secondary levels, they are more ready to accept and work together with children with SEN. On the whole, providing an environment for typically developing children to study together with children with SEN provides an opportunity for them to observe and learn more about the specials needs of their peers.

Diamond et al. (1997) found that there is a link between the experiences children have with people with disabilities and their general perceptions of disabilities. Their research involved making comparisons between children in an inclusive setting and those who were not. It was observed that the former group had higher acceptance level of people with disabilities than the latter group. In addition to this conclusion, Diamond et al. (1997) also found that the former group also had better acceptance of all their classmates. This shows that being exposed to an inclusive educational setting at the preschool level does have long-term benefits for children in terms of their sensitivity and understanding of people with disability. This view is supported by the findings of a study carried out in Uganda. Eighty-eight students without special needs, studying in an inclusive environment, were interviewed. All of them felt that they were generally contented with attending classes with children with SEN (Kristensen, 2002). Again, this Ugandan research strongly suggests that having SEN children studying together with typically developing children can become a reality if the teachers and students can have better knowledge about the range of special needs in their context as well as have some ideas on the ways to handle their situation.

A range of studies has found that interpersonal relationships formed at preschool are instrumental in the character formation and empathy of young children (Erwin et al., 1999). In more ways than one, an inclusive educational setting paves the way for cultivating social competence (Nabors, 1997b). Nabors' study in the US involved a mixed group of 59 preschool children consisting of both typically developing as well as children with SEN. The objective of the study was to investigate the playmate choice of each child in response to questions pertaining to the nomination of peers. It was observed that children with SEN were not the immediate playmate choices though they were not openly rejected. This implies that there were insufficient opportunities for all children to be involved in cooperative play activities collectively. This conclusion points to the relationship between the social play setting available in the classroom and its implications for this study. Likewise, Costenbader (2000) found through observations of inclusive preschool classrooms that there is a positive outcome in the level of interaction with peers as well as the quality of play activities among children. As noted by Ivory and McCollum (1999), social play is an important means of supporting the development of language, social, cognitive, and emotional development. Ivory and McCollum (1999) conducted a study in the US involving eight children with SEN in two different inclusive preschool settings. They observed the children during free play and noted that the children preferred parallel play with little peer communication. Another study in the US with a similar objective was conducted by Wolfberg and Schuber (1999) and it was found that generally, children with SEN were keen on social play, there was a range of brief to frequent interactions.

The discussion so far has focused on the connection between social interaction and the general level of acceptance of children with SEN. This is of interest to current researchers because the findings shed light on how to create conducive learning environments that promote academic and social development of children with SEN.

One of the ways to encourage communication for children with SEN who are non-verbal, is to use the PECS System (Picture Exchange Comunication System) (Bondy, 2001). Using the PECS could encourage better sharing of things among children as there is a communication tool available for them to use. According to Garfinkle and Schwartz (1996), children become familiar with various ways in which messages can be delivered and social contact established. PECS has been found to be beneficial in allowing children with SEN to function independently and to allow them to exert control over their environment. One way this has been used in preschools is by giving "picture schedules that indicate the sequence of daily activities and, often, the sequence of events within activities" (Hains et al., 1989).

2.5 Support for teachers in managing children with special needs

From the empirical review of literature, it has been noted that there is insufficient support to develop a separate pedagogy for special needs

(Davis & Florian, 2004; Lewis & Norwich, 2005). Booth and Ainscow (2000) believe that teachers need to be given the support they need so that they can challenge themselves by probing further effective possibilities of ensuring education for all children. On the whole, the level of support that teachers are given affects the educational policy implemented in various settings. Thus, these thoughts lead to the formation of the fourth research question, that which looks into the level of support given to teachers and expected by teachers in managing children with SEN in their classes.

One of the factors is the level of support teachers receive in their current situation. Clough and Lindsay (1991) noted that there could be some variations in the level of support teachers receive in various countries or states. Support can come in the form of funding, special needs teacher aides, educational psychologists, peers and principals. When some of these supports are not sufficiently available to teachers, they may feel anxious, incompetent, or even fearful in managing children with SEN in mainstream classes.

Bannister et al. (1998) conducted a survey among mainstream teachers in south-west England where there had been significant developments over the previous few years to understand what teachers felt about having to teach children with SEN in mainstream classes. The survey questions that were used are somewhat similar to those used in my study, in the sense that they pertained to teachers' perceptions of having children with SEN in their mainstream classes as well as the level of training they have to deal confidently with their situation. Bannister et al. (1998) examined the level of support available for teachers in an inclusive educational setting and found that there was generally a positive perception among teachers in having children with SEN in the classes. However, it was also found that children who had emotional and behavioural difficulties were seen as more difficult to manage than other types of special needs. Furthermore, teachers who had taught previously in an inclusive educational setting were more positive in their views about children with SEN. Another significant finding was that the greater the level of professional training the teachers had was closely related to their perceptions of managing children with SEN. Those who had sufficient training were more confident in dealing with children with SEN in mainstream classes.

Analysis of the data in the Bannister study pointed to three main factors that affected the perception of these teachers. They were the level of support, the level of training and the resources available to them (Bannister et al., 1998). As noted above, these were some of the same factors investigated in my study. The last guiding question of my study sought to establish the kind of support that teachers expected to receive in order to manage children with SEN confidently in mainstream classes.

While it is becoming common practice in many countries to include children with SEN in mainstream classes, it is essential that teachers are equipped with the necessary knowledge and training in dealing with these children. As mentioned above, generally, teachers felt more competent to manage these children if they had prior experience or training in this area. This is understandable as with necessary resources available, teachers would be better prepared to handle the situation. Hence, teacher training courses should include skills which are upgraded to match the current trends in managing children with SEN in mainstream classes. Research in this field suggests that with resources and training available to support teachers who have children with SEN in mainstream classes, teachers would be able to take on the challenge of dealing with their situation. This view is supported by Kristensen (2002) who believes strongly that the support system should be able to provide sustained and reliable advice to teachers and students so that there can be quality education. He agrees that while it is important for teachers to have a positive attitude towards and knowledge of inclusive education, it is also essential that they have sufficient training so that they can handle a diverse range of students in the same class. He emphasizes the need for teachers to undergo continuous training in special needs education.

Kristensen (2002) reviewed the study done on teachers in Uganda which looked into what teachers felt as the most common issues in managing children with SEN in mainstream classes. The teachers involved in the study felt that there were insufficient educational resources, insufficient information about inclusive educational setting, insufficient strategies to teach children with specific impairments, rather high ratio between teacher and students and inadequate time allocation for children with SEN (Kristensen, 2002). These findings do have some relevance to the situation in Singapore as the teachers here deal with similar situations in their day-to-day teaching job.

Another element of gauging support for teachers in an inclusive educational setting would be the level of monitoring and follow-up actions that ensue after the assessment. Supervisors of the preschools or personnel of higher authority such as the Ministry of Education and MCYS periodically monitor the operation and implementation of specific programmes. This is to assist preschools to assess their current practices and re-think their goals in order for improvements to be made to the existing programmes at the preschools. According to Retas and Kwan (2000), the term 'quality' refers to "the features of environment and experience that are presumed to be beneficial to the children's development and well-being" (Retas & Kwan, 2000:54). In view of this statement, the physical layout as well as the activities that are carried out in the preschools would have to be regularly monitored for possible changes that will enhance the learning experience as well as the overall growth of the children. When the need arises, the teachers and the management committees of the preschools can modify current practices according to the needs of the children.

One important area of improvement could be teacher training. Appropriate teacher training affects the quality of the programme run in preschools and this is connected to good results for the children (Retas & Kwan, 2000, p. 56). Hence, if teachers were given opportunities to constantly upgrade their skills in management and hone their knowledge in pedagogies, in the long run, this would benefit the children.

Singapore has a meritocratic system with much emphasis on academic achievement. This means that there would naturally be a high expectation on the preschools to focus on academic programmes. This may be different from what the preschool professionals would expect in terms of quality education which encompasses social, emotional, moral, cognitive and literacy and physical development of the child. Hence, the school teaching staff and the management committee would have to come to an agreement as to what quality education entails in that particular preschool. In an inclusive preschool setting, this would mean that the teachers involved should have a clear understanding of the needs of the children in their preschool before carrying out the suggested programmes. Then, when the activities are carried out, they would be in a better position to observe the implementation and modifications needed to make the programme an effective one. From this point, it would be easier for the management committee to assist the teachers by providing the necessary support needed.

Many of the studies cited in this literature review focus on preschool settings in the United States of America (US). Some background information to the education system in the US would be useful at this point to see the current discussion in perspective. In the United States, there are no mandatory preschool education programs, and there are very few state funded preschool institutions (www.schome.ac.uk/wiki). There is the 'Head Start' program catering to children from low-income families and this is funded by the state. This program aims to prepare children under the age of five for school. Most children in America spend the first five or six years of education in Elementary School. Children attend kindergarten in the first year of Elementary School and this is in fact not compulsory in most states. While in kindergarten children gain basic education in English, Mathematics, History, Science, Art and Music although the last three are not the main focus. At the ages of ten to eleven, children go up to Middle School, or Junior High and this can vary between states. At this stage, students can opt for the subjects they want to study. Lessons are conducted in different rooms and students move from class to class according to their timetable. This is different from the Elementary School whereby lessons are basically taught in the same room and mostly by the same teacher.

Based on this information, it appears that the education system in the US allows more flexibility in carrying out processes as there are variations in the way the system in managed in various districts. In

Singapore, the school day in most pre-schools is structured such that children stay in one room and are taught by the same teacher except for some subjects like Mother-Tongue and Music, whereby they go to special designated classrooms. Therefore, the feasibility of the strategies used in the classrooms which included children with SEN as seen in the US may differ in Singapore's context as there are some structural and differences. Hence, this study is relevant to the local context in allowing us to gain an insight into the views of one small group of Singapore preschool teachers who have to manage children with SEN in mainstream classes given the classroom structural and procedural limitations.

This present study aims to identify the level of understanding teachers in one Singapore pre-school have about special needs as well as their level of readiness in dealing with these children. From the findings, it may be possible to make suggestions about what more could be done to better prepare teachers to manage children with SEN confidently in their schools. While it is heartening to note that quite an extensive level of research is available on the topic of managing preschool children with SEN in mainstream classes in other countries, this study specifically looks into the situation in Singapore.

Chapter Three:

Methodology

3.1 Introduction

This chapter provides an overview of the research plan. It provides information on the research design, strategy, data-collecting and data-analysis methods used in the study. The first section explains the strategy and design of this study. In this section, decisions on the methods used for data collection as well as some examples will be provided. Interviews and observations were used to collect data. The second section covers sampling decisions and is followed by section 3.3 on data-collection procedures. Additional information on data-collection tools is provided in section 3.5.1. In the data analysis section, the framework provided by Miles and Huberman (1994) is explored and utilized to analyse the data collected. This explains the steps of data display, data reduction and drawing and verifying conclusions. The final section of this chapter deals with the ethical considerations taken into account while carrying out this research.

3.2 Strategy and Design

This section will explain the strategy and design of this study. A qualitative study utilizing the case study design was used to carry out the research. The purpose of adopting a qualitative (phenomenological) research approach rather than a quantitative one was because I wished to explore the perspectives of preschool teachers with regards to how they manage children with special needs in their classes. The case study design was selected as the one suitable for the present study because it serves the purpose of facilitating an in-depth investigation which is also holistic (Feagin, Orum & Sjoberg, 1991). Case studies enable researchers to highlight certain details which may be hidden in other forms of research design. Hence, a thorough understanding of the phenomenon under study was possible through a case study. Among the three kinds of case studies identified by Yin (2003), exploratory, explanatory and descriptive, this study would come under the type exploratory because it explores the strategies used by teachers in managing children with SEN in their classes. Among the three other types of case studies indicated by Stake (1995), intrinsic, instrumental and descriptive, the present study would be both instrumental and intrinsic. The case study is instrumental in nature as it serves to shed light on something which may not be well understood by the researcher. It would be intrinsic too because as an educator, I have an interest in the case being studied.

This research involves an intrinsic case study, carried out to have a better understanding of a particular case. According to Yin (2003), a case study is used to investigate a current phenomenon in its real-life context. This study involved examining the views of pre-school teachers with regards to inclusion from the point of view of the practitioners. This means that first hand information was derived from the people who are directly involved in the phenomenon being studied, i.e. inclusive pre-school education. This study was also carried out in the context where the issue being explored is practiced in the classroom.

The purpose of this study is to understand the phenomenon in depth, in its specific context (Stake, 1995). The findings, however, from this study may possibly be applied to other similar cases (Punch, 2005). This is in accordance with what Firestone (1993) claims that case-to-case transfer is possible when we talk about generalizability. What is meant here is the transfer of knowledge obtained from one case which can be applied to another similar case. Yin (2003) further supports this by referring to the term 'analytical generalization' whereby the theory that has been developed at any one point can be compared to the results of another empirical case study. Thus, the case study does not stand in isolation without relevance to other case studies. Instead, the findings of the study may be compared to others of a similar nature.

The central research question of this study was as follows:

> *In a preschool in Singapore that accepts children with special needs, how do teachers manage these children in their classes in the first six months of doing so?*

The study regarding the perspectives of preschool teachers on managing children with special needs was guided by the following four questions:

1. What are the teachers' general views about having children with special needs in their classes?
2. What educational strategies are implemented by the teacher in the classroom to accommodate children with special needs?
3. How do teachers encourage the rest of the children in the class to accept children with special needs?
4. What kind of support do teachers expect to get from the school management committee in order to manage children with special needs?

3.3 Population and sampling

Originally, I wanted to carry out the research on a number of schools so that a certain level of comparison would be possible. However, except for the school that has been presented in this chapter, the other schools rejected my approach as they were concerned that their participation in the study might result in adverse reporting which would in turn affect their credibility as a school. Hence, due to the lack of cooperation from the other schools I approached, only one school was involved in this study.

The population for this study is defined as all the teachers teaching in PCS childcare centre integrated programme. The reason for selecting all the teachers in this preschool to participate in this study is that there should be a fair representation of teachers teaching different age and grade levels of students in order to gather information based on their wide range of experience. The results of this study will be useful to teachers teaching children with SEN in mainstream educational settings, that is, alongside other typically developing children.

Sampling decisions were made based on the guidelines provided by Miles and Huberman (1994). The following checklist was closely referred to when the sampling plan was constructed:

- Is the sampling relevant to your conceptual frame and research questions?
- Will the phenomena you are interested in appear? In principle, can they appear?
- Does your plan enhance generalizability of your findings, through either conceptual power or representativeness?
- Can believeable descriptions and explanations be produced, ones that are true to real life?
- Is the sampling plan feasible, in terms of time, money, access to people and your own work style?
- Is the sampling plan ethical, in terms of such issues as informed consent, potential benefits and risk, and the relationships with informants?

I attempted to answer the above six questions to ensure that my sampling population served my purpose. The study population comprised 8 teachers from a pre-school in the Eastern district of Singapore. All the participants of this study teach mainstream children as well as deal with children with special needs in their classes. Besides the core training, teachers also participate in in-house and external enrichment workshops on topics such as Music and Movement, storytelling, classroom activities to enhance phonemic awareness, teacher-child interaction and awareness in Multiple Intelligences. Other than the pre-service training put in place, the teachers also continue to attend in-service refresher workshops. The teachers taught the playgroup, nursery and kindergarten 1 and 2 classes. Thus, it was possible to cover a wide range of teachers whose experiences could also vary according to the level of children they deal with in their classes.

Next, I believed that the phenomenon I was interested in would appear because all the teachers who participated in the study were from different classes and taught both children with SEN as well as typically developing children. Hence, with their spectrum of experiences with different cohorts of children, their responses would be able to describe the situation from their perspective. Thirdly, my research plan does not aim to generalize any observations but to describe the phenomena in its unique context. The findings of this case study may not be representative of all similar contexts. Believable descriptions and explanations that are true to real life can be produced as they are based on authentic data collected in real classroom situations involving actual participants. The sampling plan was feasible, in terms of time, money and access to people and my own work style because prior arrangements were made with the preschool principal and teachers to ensure that they were available for the interviewing sessions as well as the observation sessions. Hence, the time and costs involved were assessed well prior to the actual data collection sessions. Furthermore, the participants were cooperative with regards to matching their schedules with mine. Thus, it was feasible to carry out the data-collection as planned. Lastly, the sampling plan was ethical, in terms of such issues as informed consent, potential benefits and risk, and the relationships with informants. I contacted the participants through the principal who assisted in arranging the slots for the respective data-collection schedules. Participants were given detailed information about the study and other information pertaining to the contact details of my supervisor and myself should they need further clarification. Signed agreement was obtained from each participant prior to the interview sessions.

3.4 Ethical Considerations

As requested by the principal of the preschool, information pertaining to the participants was kept confidential and their names were not reflected in any part of the dissertation. None of the children who were present during the data-collection procedures were identified either. As also promised prior to the study, their pictures were not used, nor were they recognizable by any other form of documentation. Their recorded interviews were stored in a safe cabinet and used only for transcribing purposes. In addition, an ethical clearance form was filled up and submitted to The University of Western Australia's Examination Board for approval. Data collection began after obtaining the approval from the respective authority from the university.

3.5 Data Collection

Permission was obtained from the preschool to implement the qualitative study through e-mails to the managing director as well as the centre principal. This was followed by phone calls which served to assure the respective parties of confidentiality of the participants as well as give further details of the actual data collection method. Teachers read through the aims of the study as well as other details and references and signed a written agreement that ensured confidentiality of information obtained during the data-gathering process. Throughout the study, participants were assured of keeping their identity anonymous. Participants were kept informed through the transcription of the interview sessions in order to assure them that none of the information is false but as was obtained during the interview sessions.

The research questions to be investigated, the available resources, as well as the timeline were taken into consideration when conducting the study. In addition to these considerations, triangulation, which involves combining various methods of data collection, would ensure reliability of the findings of the research. In view of this, data collection methods consisted of semi-structured interviews and classroom observations. These tools of data collection were used for triangulation purposes. By using more than a single source of evidence, it is possible to avoid a tunnel vision which can narrow the researcher's perspective rather than provide a wider scope (Verschuren, 2003). Yin (2003) also suggests keeping a collection of evidence in sequence, in order to ensure reliability of the information. By comparing data derived from both modes, it would be possible to look for patterns emerging and arrive as conclusions about the research topic.

The data collection process followed the guidelines provided by Punch (2005). The main issues taken into consideration were sample selection, management of the interview sessions and recording. The pertinent points considered were as follows:

- Who will be interviewed and why?
- How many will be interviewed, and how many times will each person be interviewed?
- When and for how long will each respondent be interviewed?
- Where will each respondent be interviewed?
- How will access to the interview situation be organized?

(Punch, 2005)

3.6 Time frame

Three interview sessions took place. The first round of interviews was conducted in January, 2008. This was followed by the first observation made in February. After this, the second set of interviews were conducted in March, 2008. In April, the second observation was made. In May, 2008, the third interview session was carried out. In June, the third observation was made. The next section provides some information about the data collection tools that were used and why they were appropriate to my research.

3.7 Instrumentation: Semi-structured Interviews

Semi-structured interviews were used to collect data in this study. This was done to allow participants to give their perspectives on managing children with SEN in mainstream classroom setting. Using interviews to collect qualitative data provides a situation whereby the participants get to express their thoughts and feelings on a given topic. The subject matter is decided by the person conducting the research and the way the interview unfolds is dependent on the responses that appear in the process of the interview and further questions asked by the interviewer.

The purpose of using the semi-structured interview is to gain an understanding of the phenomenon from the participant's perspective instead of generalizing about certain behaviour. Open-ended questions are used in this technique. While there could be some set questions, others occur during the interviewing process. Although some questions are predetermined, there are opportunities to probe further (Berg, 2004). As a result, the way questions are phrased may not be identical for all participants.

Using interviews as a data-collecting instrument allowed a positive relationship to develop between the researcher and the participants which was crucial in obtaining the latter's co-operation and honest responses to the questions asked. Furthermore, by creating a comfortable environment for the participants to engage with the researcher, the task of data collection was carried out with ease. By building trust in the participants, the researcher found the task of clarifying information more manageable as the participants were generally more forthcoming with their responses. As pointed out by Nunan (1992), in a semi-structured interview, the interviewer has a general expectation of the direction and the outcome of the interview but does not proceed with the interview with strictly prepared questions. Points raised during the course of the interview directed the course of the session. This method provided room for open-discussion of the participants' experiences. This provided opportunities for the researcher to enter the world of the participants' unique and personal experiences.

This study used semi-structured interviews as the interactions during data-gathering are rather rich and the data show significant evidence about real-life experiences (Nunan, 1992). In addition, there are three advantages of using it to collect data. Firstly, the interviewee is empowered to steer the direction of the interview. Next, there is a considerable degree of flexibility for the interviewer. Thirdly, it serves as a passport to enter other people's lives (Nunan, 1992). Therefore, the merits of the semi-structured interview mentioned above, justify its choice as a data-collection method for this study.

Furthermore, certain complex questions can be clarified by the interviewer's probing of the participants. Also, this type of data collection method is simple and practical and it is particularly useful in gathering qualitative data involving participants' thoughts and feelings about the situation they are in. Last but not least, this tool is useful in collecting data because of the convenience with which information can be stored either through video or audio recording.

While there are strengths in using semi-structured interviews, there are also some limitations to using this tool for data collection. Firstly, the process of conducting the interview depends heavily on the interviewer. He or she should have the capacity to manoeuvre the interview in such a way that the responses derived serve the objective of conducting the interviews. For this, the interviewer has to be quick in thinking and be articulate enough to form questions on the spot and encourage the participants to contribute rich information.

Another drawback of using the interview for data collection is that, at times, the interviewer might unknowingly give out signals which would steer the participants towards giving responses that are expected. Then, the responses may not be a true reflection of the participants' thoughts and feelings. When used over and over, the semi-structured interview may not yield the same results. As this tool mainly deals with obtaining participants' personal reactions to the subject matter, it would not be feasible to expect consistent results over a certain period of time. Hence, it may not be a reliable data collection tool.

As this study involves gathering qualitative data, it could be cumbersome to differentiate what is reliable and what is not. Also, as the interview involves personal feelings, it would be difficult to make generalizations about the participants' responses. Last but not least, the truthfulness of the responses cannot be assured. There is no way of measuring the level of honesty involved in the responses given by the participants.

3.8 Validity

Validity refers to how accurate or truthful a measurement is. It answers the question of whether we are measuring what we think we are measuring. While there is no statistical test to assess validity, it is based mainly on the subjectivity of the researcher. So, by using semi-structured interviews the participants are able to express their viewpoints in detail and explore the topic in depth. During the interview session they are able to have the freedom to express their thoughts without much interference of the interviewer.

3.9 Reliability

Reliability is one aspect that determines the quality of measurement used in a research. Simply put, reliability refers to the extent to which the same experiment can be carried out again using the same instruments and still obtain consistent results (Trochim, 2000). In that sense, this study is reliable given the context and the nature of the research. If a similar study were to be carried out in another preschool, it would be possible to measure the deliverables as specified in the research question.

3.10 Procedure

The interview was managed using the checklist provided by Punch (2005) which was as follows:

- Preparation for the interview: the interview schedule
- Beginning the interview: establishing rapport
- Communication and listening skills
- Asking questions: the sequence and types of questions
- Closing the interview

A timetable was drawn up to fit in the two types of data collection sessions in an alternative sequence. A month's break was given between the first type of data collection and the next so that the participants had sufficient time to display changes in their responses, if any. Intermittently, the participants allowed me to make informal observations on an ad hoc basis. So, I made arrangements by phone to let them know that I would be present at specific times at specific locations to observe the activities and behaviour of the children as well as the teachers. The teachers were cooperative and agreed to this request. Hence, I was able to take more field notes as and when my free time permitted. I sent a timetable stating my data collection schedule by electronic mail to the preschool principal who then passed this information to the respective teachers. As such, there were occasions when I had to make more trips to the centre for the interview sessions as, at some points, one or two teachers were absent from work due to medical reasons.

Prior to the start of each interview, I introduced myself and briefly told the participants my purpose of the study and being in that location. This was to help them feel comfortable and to gain their confidence in me. The aim was to make them less nervous and more at ease. After establishing rapport with the participants, I showed them a paper containing the main questions that I would be asking so that they had some time to think about their experiences and provide responses that would be a true reflection of what they actually thought and experienced.

Three rounds of interviews were conducted. The first one was conducted at the beginning of the school year in January, 2008 to find out the initial thoughts of teachers (regarding the inclusion of children with special needs in their classes and their intended strategies for managing children with SEN together with other typically developing children) when they were assigned their respective classes for the year. The questions asked during the first interview are in Appendix 1. The first interview question sought to find out more about the teacher's initial reaction when they were told that they would be teaching a class comprising children with special needs. The next question aimed to explore how the teacher actually implemented teaching strategies in a class which has children with SEN and other typically developing children. In addition, the teacher was also invited to share some of the challenges they could have faced in the given situation and how they managed them. The third question dealt with investigating the level of acceptance of other typically developing children with regards to the children with special needs. The fourth interview question served to get responses about any additional support the teachers wished to get so that they could manage their classroom situation better. For this question, some teachers were not able to answer immediately as they were not sure what was expected of them. Then, the researcher gave some examples of support like manpower, materials and training after which the participants were able to elaborate on their answers.

The second interview was carried out two months later in March, 2008. This was done in order to track the thoughts of the participants from the beginning to that point in time and take note of the changes in perspectives that emerged along the way. The questions asked during the second interview are in Appendix 2. Each of the questions used in the second interview corresponded to the guiding questions stated above.

The third interview session was conducted two months after the second session in May, 2008. The questions asked during the third interview are in Appendix 3. These questions served to track the changes in the thoughts and feeling of the teachers in the inclusive setting in managing children with special needs and they are in line with the guiding questions provided in the earlier part of this section.

From the first interview session, participants' expectations and concerns for the rest of the year with regards to managing children with SEN in mainstream classroom settings were noted. This was then compared to the second session of interview and was a rich source of data for collecting information on the strategies that have been used and their reactions and changes to them during the months between the first and the last interview sessions.

During the second interview, transcripts of the first interview were made available to the participants for checking purposes. Participants were requested to look through their responses to confirm that their responses were represented accurately. The second interview served to gain supplementary information which enhanced the first interview sessions as well as to gain additional information which might have been missed out in the first session. It also allowed the researcher to follow-up on perceptions which may have changed during the time lapse between interview sessions. After the second interview, transcripts were made available to the participants to verify its contents and to confirm its correct representation by signing on the transcript. Although the exact wording may differ, the general concepts discussed were presented as close as possible to the actual interaction that took place during the interview session.

Throughout the interview, we sat in a quiet room whereby there was very little noise interference as I was audio recording the interview sessions. At the same time, I was also taking short notes. Initially, I stated the major question for which the participants responded accordingly. At times, when they were pausing, I asked further guiding questions so that they were clear about what I wanted to know. Hence, the interview session per participant lasted approximately one hour or even more for some who had more observations to share with me. Throughout, I listened attentively without much interference. I spoke only when I needed further explanation or clarification of the information given. The interview sessions proceeded smoothly as the informality of the atmosphere allowed the participants to express their views freely without being self-conscious about being watched or heard by any other person other than me. As I had assured the participants of confidentiality, they were most cooperative with me and were willing to contribute their thoughts and feelings freely. At the close of the interview, I summarized the participants' main responses during the interview and thanked them for assisting in the data collection procedure. I also told them when I would be making a visit to the centre again to conduct observations and the subsequent interview sessions.

3.11 Recording

Electronic audio-recording was used. The first interview was carried out in an enclosed environment, in an office. This made it possible to block out noise which would otherwise interfere with the clear recording of the interview. The second interview, however, took place in a corner of the pre-school classroom when the children were taking their afternoon nap. The quiet office was not available on the second interview day. Thus, during the recording, there were a few interruptions, such as children talking to the teacher and other teachers' movement in that area. Although the voice recording was not so clear at some points, the researcher managed to ask more questions to clarify the points raised. The third interview took place like the second and the same interferences were present. Yet, the interview went as planned and the respondents answered all the questions given.

3.12 Instrumentation: Observations

As pointed out by Punch (2005), the point of a qualitative study is "to look at something holistically and comprehensively, to study it in its complexity, and to understand it in its context" (Punch, 2005:186). Keeping this in mind, classroom observation was carried out as a follow-up to interview sessions. The observation was conducted to seek out similarities and/or differences between what the teachers said and did in actual classroom lessons. From the observations made, subsequent interview questions were modified so that doubts, or issues noted, could be clarified with the teachers concerned. For example, when one child with special needs could not follow the story told by one teacher, another teacher took him aside and did a simplified reading lesson with him. In the next interview, this was brought up and the teacher was asked why she did that and whether that child could follow the modified lesson from then onwards.

As a data-collection method, observation has been widely used by educational researchers because they are contextual and done in real time (Yin, 2003). As observation involves noting behaviour visually as well as through listening, the researcher is able to gather useful data through this mode. In qualitative data collection, observation is carried out in "a more natural open-ended way" (Punch, 2005). During the process of observation, actions and events are allowed to occur naturally while they are observed and recorded. In this research, unstructured observation was used as it was intended to look at a holistic behaviour pattern without any modification to actual classroom practices. As the school leader was assured that no video-recording would take place, note-taking on paper was done.

Observations were carried out after each of the three interview sessions respectively in February, April and June. Each observation was made for thirty minutes. The researcher was observing the teacher's reaction to the children with special needs while she conducted the lesson, the strategies used to manage the children with special needs alongside their peers, and the ways in which the teacher encouraged the other typically developing children to accept and include the children with special needs in their group activities. These three elements relate to the first three research questions mentioned at the beginning of this chapter, namely, the teachers' attitude towards children with SEN, strategies used to manage them in an inclusive classroom as well as tracking the level of acceptance of this by typically developing children.

Through the observations, the researcher was able to clarify points that arose after carrying out the initial interview sessions. This included the teacher's reaction to learning demands or behaviour issues that came up in the midst of the lesson pertaining to children with special needs. By actually being present in the environment where the action takes place, i.e. the classroom, the researcher was able to see the strategies employed in dealing with children with special needs in real classroom situations.

3.13 Data analysis

In this study, Miles & Huberman's (1994) framework was used for analyzing qualitative data. This was most appropriate as this study involved an interpretivist attempt to understand behaviour and thought processes that encourage a particular behaviour through words rather than numerical representation.

The interview questions served to narrow down the focus to specific areas of concern and allowed better expression of respondents' thoughts and feelings about inclusion. For example, the participants were given a platform to express their initial thoughts and feelings when they were faced with an inclusive classroom. From this point, they were further encouraged to talk about their needs in preparing themselves to deal better with an inclusive situation. The information obtained was presented through flow charts and diagrams and written descriptions. This was done in accordance with suggestions by Miles and Huberman (1994) whereby data was displayed and reduced. According to these researchers, data display serves to "assemble and organize information in an immediately accessible, compact form, so that the analyst can see what is happening and either draw justified conclusions or move on to the next-step analysis which the display suggests may be useful (Miles and Huberman, 1994). While this was done in a rather straightforward manner by presenting the data that was collected, the next step was challenging.

Data reduction involved leaving out what seemed to be less pertinent and sieving out what directly enhanced the understanding of the case under study. This process, however, could be subjective as it might seem that all data were indeed relevant and the researcher had some difficulty in deciding on the data that could be left out. Since the amount of data gathered was considerable, the researcher was challenged with the task of reducing it all into a shorter version. If this step was not carried out correctly, it would be possible to produce an inaccurate understanding of the data. Although qualitative research tends to deal less with numerical analysis than quantitative research, there is a certain level of assigning numeric value when deciding which information is significant depending on the number of times a particular behaviour is observed in response to a particular event. As mentioned by Miles and Huberman (1994), "The moment we say something is 'important' or 'significant' or 'recurrent', we have achieved that estimate in part by making counts, comparisons and weights" (Miles and Huberman, 1994, p.215). Hence, numerical values did appear in this research although not to the extent of their occurrence in quantitative research.

In accordance with Miles and Huberman (1994), coding and memoing were utilized to label data according to certain categories. Coding involved attaching tags, names or labels to parts of data so that the researcher was able to have a better understanding of the data as she would be able to make meaning of it better. These tools helped to store and retrieve data in specific categories. There were three levels of coding. The first level of coding served to describe and summarise parts of data which were relevant for advanced coding later, when inference of data took place. At the next level, the researcher focused on pattern codes by gathering codes into more meaningful units. Next, less abstract and more descriptive codes were brought together to form a more abstract concept (Punch, 2005). From this initial step, advance coding allowed themes to emerge which led to the identification of patterns (Punch, 2005). Alongside coding the process of memoing occurred. This involved recording ideas in the process of analyzing data. This allowed the researcher to record important ideas which occurred while coding, which was when the researcher paused the coding task and wrote down thoughts which occurred at that point. Examples of codes were the recurrence of terms like 'need' and 'problems'. These drew the researcher's attention to possible changes that could be made to current practices that would improve the present situation in that pre-school.

In coding, some of the tags were 'ok', 'difficult', 'include', 'together' and 'help'. I used these tags to summarise the general situation faced by the participants. If they felt that something was manageable, they usually said 'ok'. The word 'difficult' was tagged when they found some aspects unmanageable or could be managed with difficulty. The word 'include' and 'together' were tagged to refer to inclusive behaviour. When it came to memoing, some important thoughts arose, such as, when the participant mentioned 'external party involvement'. This signals another need of the participant besides those that were anticipated in the interview sessions. For example, some participants mentioned getting therapists to come down to the centre on a regular basis to monitor the progress of the children and provide therapy sessions accordingly. Another participant mentioned the need for the inclusion specialist to come to the centre more regularly and assist the teachers in their efforts to manage an inclusive teaching and learning environment. These points were important and were noted down as leading pathways for further research in this area.

The third stage involved drawing conclusions and verifying findings. This was the stage where patterns that emerged were noted and inconsistencies explained. It involved making meaning from collected data and verifying conclusions. In Miles and Hubermans' (1994) words, the researcher was then challenged to "find the outliers, then verify whether what is present in them is absent or different in other, more mainstream examples" (Miles and Huberman, 1994, p.237). If there was information that did not tally with the rest of the general findings, the researcher was given an indication of the areas that needed further research to get an in-depth understanding of the inconsistencies.

3.14 Assumptions of the research

One assumption is that the semi-structured interviews and the observations are valid and reliable tools of data-collection. I also assume that the participants would be truthful in their responses although there is no way I could confirm this. Hence, my findings are entirely based on the responses derived from the participants.

In summary, this chapter explained the research design of this study, the data collection decisions, the procedures as well as the data analysis method that was utilized in this study. The findings of the study are discussed in the next chapter.

Chapter Four:

Findings

4.1 Introduction

This chapter reports on the results from the data collected and analysed in the course of this study. Two modes of data collection were carried out over a span of six months: 3 semi-structured interviews with each teacher and 3 observations of each teacher. The main objective of carrying out the study was to find out how preschool teachers manage children with special needs in their classrooms. Miles and Huberman's (1994) framework was used to analyse the data collected. The main components of this framework are data display, data reduction and drawing and verifying conclusions. First the raw data were recorded. After that the data was narrowed down to focus on those that were pertinent to the research questions of this study through coding and memoing. Next, conclusions were drawn and verified by looking out for recurring patterns in the data. This chapter reports on the findings from the data and these are compared with the literature reviewed in chapter two to look out for consistencies and discrepancies. These will be discussed further in chapter 5.

4.2 Background information of classes participating in study

The Nursery class had 15 children in total ranging from 3 to 4 years old. There was one child with special needs in this class. The Kindergarten 1 class had 11 children in total ranging from 4 to 5 years old. There were 2 children with special needs in this class. The Kindergarten 2 class had 18 children ranging from 5 to 6 years old. There were three children with special needs in this class. Mainly, the children with special needs had Autism and/or Attention Deficit Disorder.

4.3 Teachers' general views about including children with SEN in their classes

The data collected was further classified through coding in which statements which had a common thread running through them were grouped together. A sample of the coding process is provided below.

Table 1: Unordered List of Responses to the Open-Ended Question:
What are your general views about having children with special needs in your class?

Participant Responses
I am a little hesitant about having children with special needs in my class.
It would not be easy to handle children with special needs.
I do not know much about children with special needs.
I do not have the confidence to manage children with special needs.
I think children with special needs should be sent to special schools where the lessons are catered to their specific needs.
After going for training, I feel more confident in dealing with children with special needs.
It is a good idea to have children with special needs learn together with other typically developing children. This will create empathy and awareness among typically developing children about the differences and/or difficulties faced by children with special needs.

I was not surprised or taken aback when I realized that I would be teaching children with special needs as I have the experience of volunteering in organizations involving children with special needs.

I feel pity for children with special needs because they cannot do things like other typically developing children.

Children with special needs can also be trained to do many things if proper structure and training for teachers is in place.

Children can learn to do more things with extra time and flexibility in their learning programme.

I am concerned about dividing teaching time between children with special needs and typically developing children.

Gradually, I feel more comfortable teaching children with special needs as my mindset has become more positive.

I focus on the strengths of children with special needs.

Table 1.2: Categorization of Responses to the Open-Ended Question: What are your views about having children with special needs in your class?

Inductive Categories	Participant Responses
Anxiety	I am a little hesitant about having children with special needs in my class. It would not be easy to handle children with special needs.
Incompetence	I do not know much about children with special needs. I do not have the confidence to manage children with special needs. I am concerned about dividing teaching time between children with special needs and typically developing children.
Negative mindset	I think children with special needs should be sent to special schools where the lessons are catered to their specific needs.

	I feel pity for children with special needs because they cannot do things like other typically developing children.
Positive mindset	After going for training, I feel more confident in dealing with children with special needs. It is a good idea to have children with special needs learn together with other typically developing children. This will create empathy and awareness among typically developing children about the differences and/or difficulties faced by children with special needs. I was not surprised or taken aback when I realized that I would be teaching children with special needs as I have the experience of volunteering in organizations involving children with special needs. Children with special needs can also be trained to do many things if proper structure and training for teachers is in place. Children can learn to do more things with extra time and flexibility in their learning programme. Gradually, I feel more comfortable teaching children with special needs as my mindset has become more positive. I focus on the strengths of children with special needs.

4.4 Effects of training and / or experience on the confidence level of teachers

Generally, although the participants felt incompetent at the earlier stage of joining the preschool, their confidence level rose after attending the ICCP course. Their understanding of children with special needs improved and they had more confidence in managing them better with the help of their colleagues. Kristensen (2002) is of the opinion that with increased awareness of their role in managing a class with a child with SEN, teachers believe in their own capability in dealing with their situation. The course they had attended covered ways to handle children with SEN, strategies to modify lessons to cater to the needs of the children in their classes and also certain boundaries that have to be taken into consideration. This is in line with Sparling's (2002) study where teachers felt positive about having children with SEN in their classes but felt daunted by their lack pf training or experience in that area.

The participants said that it was a good idea to have children with SEN in the same educational environment as other typically developing children because this would send the message that everyone is not the same and that we should appreciate one another's uniqueness. They added that such a school system would create awareness among the children about the differences and/or difficulties faced by children with SEN. Mastropieri and Scrubbs (2004) also believed that when typically developing children study in the same environment as their peers with SEN, the former's sense of empathy develops over time and they are more tolerant of the differences among them.

In terms of the participants' ability to manage these children with SEN, it was mentioned that their task was getting more manageable as the children were gradually adapting to the environment and had made more friends over time. They were also more compliant with instructions from teachers. Overall, managing the children with SEN got better as the children were able to comprehend the teachers' instructions and show better cooperation with them.

On the whole, the participants said that they were more comfortable dealing with children with special needs in the middle of the year than at the beginning of the year. This was mainly because they had a better understanding of the children's needs and were better prepared to manage unforeseen circumstances. The teachers were able to see a change in their own mindsets because they were more positive in their outlook and were able to focus on the strength of each child rather than the negative factors. As pointed out by Hargreaves (2003), teachers viewed their situation has a direct impact on the ways they handle their students and the strategies used in imparting knowledge to them.

4.5 Apprehensiveness towards having children with SEN

One participant strongly felt that children with SEN should be sent to special schools. Her reasons for this belief reiterate the views of Freire and Cesar (2002) who believe that children with SEN would benefit more from a system that specifically caters to their specific needs. In fact, Kristensen et al. (2006) make references to Uganda where resources are properly utilized for the focused care needed to be given to children with special needs.

When participants were asked about children with SEN they said that initially they were a little hesitant and thought that it would not be easy to handle them. This was because they had little knowledge of the kinds of special needs these children had and were not confident if they could manage the situation. They said that they were a little worried as to how they were going to teach typically developing children and yet spend time coaching children with SEN. This concern is similar to that found by Wilmore (1995) whereby some teachers found it difficult to look after children with SEN while devoting time to the rest of their typically developing classmates. This was gradually alleviated when the other teachers shared their knowledge and worked together as a team. Some participants felt pity for children with SEN because they felt that these children would not be able to do many things like their peers. But gradually, they began to accept that children with SEN can also do many things but just that they need more time and structure to carry out certain tasks.

Although participants did feel some level of anxiety and uncertainty regarding the challenges that were ahead of them, with the assistance of their colleagues and with improved understanding on the part of the children themselves, the task of managing the children got better over time.

4.6 Strategies used to manage children with SEN

As a normal practice, the teachers observed the child with SEN for about a week and gauged his cognitive level. Then, while teaching the class as a whole, they noted if he could cope with the lesson and changed it accordingly if he could not. In terms of assisting a child with SEN who could be slow in following instructions, the teachers simplified instructions and broke down the steps into more manageable parts. Furthermore, there was the buddy system, which involved partnering a typically developing child with a child who needed more guidance in class. In this system, the more able child explained the tasks and guided his partner to complete the tasks together. This enabled the children to complete the tasks assigned and also cultivated certain values such as compassion and teamwork in young children.

4.6.1 Time Away

Participant (P1) shared a specific strategy in dealing with children who could not sit still during lessons. She got that child to sit on a chair slightly away from his peers. In this way, the teacher believed that the child knew that his behaviour had been inappropriate and that if he wanted to join his friends, he should show good behaviour. According to P1, this method worked for her Nursery class children as no one wanted to be left out in class.

4.6.2 Buddy System

P1 also added that when the children were brought out of the preschool to the playground, the child with SEN would be partnered with a typically developing child who would assist his partner in playing outdoors. With the help of the partner the boy with SEN had been able to follow the class and walk in twos and take turns to play at the various stations. With this buddy system, the boy with SEN had shown improvement in his gross motor skills and had been able to do more activities since he joined the school.

Three participants said that their strategy depended on the teacher-student ratio. If a child's special needs were very demanding, then they would give that child personal attention when the other two teachers managed the whole class. If the child's needs were mild, then the teachers would be able to attend to the child's needs while the rest of the class activities were on-going. At the point of interview, the child with SEN was able to do basic things like untying his shoes and keeping his bag in his cubicle by himself. However, he was still in diapers and was not toilet-trained yet. So, teachers would ask him at regular intervals whether he wanted to go to the toilet. When he agreed, then the teacher would bring him to the toilet. The teachers did not use PECs because they have not been formally told to do so, nor trained to use it. So, they used verbal instructions to communicate with the child with SEN. Over time, they found that he was able to comprehend their message and act accordingly.

4.6.3 Simplified Instructions

The participants were aware that children with SEN might need to have instructions repeated and broken down into smaller and more comprehensible levels. This was one of the strategies used to make instructions understandable to children with SEN. Another strategy used was to take turns with another teacher. When one teacher teaches the regular children, the other would attend to the children with SEN. While P4 did not have any training in teaching children with SEN, her partner P5 did have some basic training in this area. P4 felt that dealing with children without any formal training was not as difficult as she thought it would be as long as she had another teacher who could assist her and share her expertise in managing these children. P6, P7 and P8 taught the class as a whole and attended to the children with SEN later when the rest of the class was occupied doing their own tasks. Giving one-to-one attention has been necessary to those children especially during art and craft sessions because the procedures needed to be simplified and modified according to the ability of the children with SEN.

4.6.4 Schedule Chart

Having a routine to follow everyday helped as the children knew what to expect next in their schedule. The timetable was enlarged and pasted on the whiteboard and after each section on the activity the teachers would question what the next activity would be. In this way the children would be mentally prepared and this would reduce any anxiety on the part of the children with SEN. Using pictures as cue cards helps to indicate tasks to children who were non-verbal. For example, when it was meal-time, the teachers would point to the picture that depicted someone eating at a table, and the child would go with his partner to the table and sit down waiting for food to be served. This applied to music time, drawing time and playtime too.

4.6.5 Time Out

One strategy was the use of "Time-out" sessions. When a child throws a tantrum, the teacher would take the child away from the classroom setting to a quiet corner and let him sit down for a while. During the few minutes he was there, he would calm down his emotions by himself, without any interruption and would join the class only when he felt ready to do so. There would be no talking on the part of the teacher. The teachers tried this method and found it helpful, as the teachers need not increase their volume to calm down the child as they felt that sometimes the child got more agitated hearing the teacher's voice. Thus, this was one of the methods that the teachers had used and found to be effective.

Most of the children were able to follow the routine of each day. However, there were some occasions when a child with or without special needs became upset and threw a tantrum. When that happened, it did disrupt the flow of the activities as the children's attention was on the child who was upset. At that point, one of the teachers would bring the child aside to a quiet place away from the whole class and let him release his frustration. If it was a typically developing child, the teacher would calm him down by getting him some tissue paper to clean his tears and assuring him that everything was alright. Then, the teacher would find out the reason for his outburst and try to tell him calmly that his reactions were inappropriate, if they were, and to tell him how his behaviour had affected his classmates. In that way, the child would be able to see the bigger consequences of his action and to be more considerate the next time he shouted or cried loudly. If the outburst came from a child with SEN, then again, the child would be removed from his class and brought aside to let him release his emotions without disturbing the rest of his classmates. After that release, the teacher would speak to the child calmly and use picture cards to indicate 'No shouting' or 'No kicking'. This was especially useful for a child who was non-verbal. After the child was more subdued, then he would be brought back to join his friends and resume his activities. The teachers also mentioned that managing a child who was non-verbal could be challenging at times because the child got more agitated at not being able to express himself as to why he was upset at that point. Hence, such situations can take a longer time to return to a calm level. It was also mentioned that when a child screams or cries, it could trigger a few children into crying. In those situations, more than one teacher would try to calm down the children by hugging them and telling them softly that everything was alright.

4.6.6 Focus on child's ability

By looking into what the children can do, the teachers were able to plan lessons that could cater to the interests of the children. This helped to keep them engaged in the activities chosen. For example, during craft work, the children were given play dough to make miniature figures of things they fancied. When the child with SEN could not stay in one place and sustain his interest in that activity, the teacher modified it by getting him to cut the play dough into smaller pieces and categorizing them into their respective coloured containers. In this way, the child was not frustrated that he could not make shapes but could do something else within his capacity. This also kept him within the group and though he was doing a different activity, he was still handing the same material and was happy to do so. This strategy was recommended by Duhaney (2004) who believed that teachers review the lesson activities and modify them according to the needs and interests of the children. This would ensure that everyone is involved in the activity within his/her own capacity. By doing this, children with SEN would be engaged in the lesson and would be less disruptive. This in turn increases the manageability of the classroom as well as ensuring that everyone is meaningfully engaged in the activities.

4.6.7 Change of Seating Position

During the observation session, I was mainly looking for strategies that the teachers used to manage children with SEN in their classes. During the story time, the teacher read a story from a big book which was placed on an easel. While reading the lines in an animated manner, the teacher was also pointing to various parts of the colourful illustration on each page. She also elicited responses from the children by pointing to certain words or phrases. While most children were able to respond to the story, the child with SEN seemed to be fidgeting as he could not sit on the floor. When the assisting teacher noticed this, she took him aside and made him sit next to her on a chair. Her close presence and the change of seating made the child feel comfortable and he was able to sit through the session. The teacher was also quietly explaining to him certain parts of the story which may be difficult for him to follow. Next, I went to the Kindergarten class for observation.

The Kindergarten 1 was having an Art and Craft session. They were making masks out of paper plates. The teachers were giving them step-by-step instructions on drawing and colouring the masks. After that, the teacher helped to punch-holes at the sides of the masks for the children to tie rubber bands which would be used to fix the masks on their faces. The child with SEN had some difficulty drawing the features of the face. The teacher assisted the child to draw the eyes, nose and mouth. When I asked why she did not get the child's buddy to help with this task, she mentioned that the buddy was also making his own mask at that time and she did not want to interrupt his involvement in the activity. However, later, she would get the buddy to fix the rubber band for the ears and help to put on the mask for his partner. The children appeared to be happily engaged in making their masks with the teachers' assistance. After this, I went to another Kindergarten class for observation.

The Kindergarten 2 was having Music time. They were using drumsticks to make music according to the rhythm of the song. Each child had a pair of drumsticks and they were used to hit on the floor with certain number of beats like "tap-tap-tap". The teacher started with simple beats initially and moved on to more complex beats later. Most of the children were able to follow the given instructions. When one child with SEN could not keep up with the pace, the teacher held his hand and showed him how to do the beats. At this point, there were two other typically developing children who lost track of the song too. Hence, their buddies helped them by showing them how to do the beats. From this it could be noted that not only do children with SEN have some difficulties following the lesson, but even regular children might not be able to keep up with the pace of their peers. Hence, the buddy system seemed to be useful for all children regardless of their capability. There was no sign of exclusion on the part of the children as they were at ease during Music time and they seemed to enjoy the session as a group.

In the Nursery class, each child was already partnered with one peer before the session. The children were listening to an audio playback of certain nursery rhymes and were following the actions of the teacher.

One such nursery song was "Head and Shoulders". In this piece, children tapped on various parts of their body according to the lines and sang the song. The teachers shared with me that through this song they reinforced their lesson on naming body parts. Throughout this session, all the children were engaged though some did at different paces. At these points, the teachers went over to hold the children's hands and guide them through the steps. There were regular children and the child with SEN who needed some help. For some songs, the partners did some steps in pairs and were able to help one another through the sequence. Hence, no one was left behind; they were either helped by a child or a teacher.

4.6.8 Alternative Learning Environment

Providing alternative learning environments was recommended by Korpan et al. (1997) who found that this encouraged better participation among the children. In addition to providing a different perspective by changing the learning environment, this move also allowed the children to reveal their hidden capabilities. The Kindergarten 1 class was brought outdoors to the playground for outdoor activities. All children were told to line up in pairs and to hold their partners' hands. They went to the playground in an orderly manner and followed the teacher's instructions. They went to each play station in pairs and played on each slide, swing and see-saw. When a child was not able to climb on a stone figure, his partner helped him along. The teacher stood close to the child with SEN while keeping a look-out for all the children as a whole. The class played a ball-throwing activity after the play session. The children stood in a big circle and numbered themselves in order. When a particular number was called, the child with the ball was supposed to throw it to that particular child. The teacher shared that through this activity, the children learned numbers and get practice in listening attentively. All the children enjoyed this play session.

The Kindergarten 2 had a cookery session. The children were each given two slices of bread. On the table were containers of lettuce, cucumbers and slices of cheese. The teachers demonstrated the steps involved in laying the ingredients in sequence and the children followed accordingly. Another teacher assisted those who were not able to follow any step. Mostly, the instructions were deliberate and clear and almost all the children were able to make their cheese sandwich. In this class too, the children helped one another in the sandwich-making session while the teacher attended to those who needed more help. The children interacted well with one another.

The Nursery class had outdoor activity. They were brought out of the preschool to a vacant space nearby and played a game. They were told to crawl through a hula-hoop, run around a triangle cone and pick up a bean bag and pass it to the next person in the group. The teachers helped the children who appeared confused as to what was to be done next. This level of assistance was what Pressley and McCormick (1995) recommended. By attending to the child who has difficulty following the lesson or completing a task, the teacher would be able to work closely with the child and monitor his / her learning process. Generally, this activity was enjoyed by all the children as guidance was provided to the children who needed extra help.

The Kindergarten 1 class had a cookery session. They were preparing vegetable salad. Each child was given a bowl and a fork. There were containers of cut vegetables and other ingredients for the salad. The teacher gave step-by-step instructions and the children obliged by doing as per instruction. At some points, when the ingredients spilled or fell off, the teacher assisted the child by guiding him through that step. Other than that, the children were encouraged to do their task independently. This was also suggested by Noonan McCormick (1993) who supports the idea of weaning off children over time from being too reliant on their teachers for task completion.

The Kindergarten 2 class had Music time. They were preparing for an upcoming concert and were practising their dance sequence for it. The children seemed rather familiar with the steps. The teacher said that they had been practising for the concert for the past 2 weeks. The steps involved the children doing certain steps in pairs. Almost all the children were doing the steps confidently. When a child forgot a step, his partner assisted him by showing the step. At times, the teacher stepped in to help out. Pressley and McCormick (1995) also favour this level of guidance, so that help is given only when the child is unable to complete a task by himself / herself. So, overall, the teacher's role was that of a facilitator who was there to assist in the learning process of the children.

From these interviews and observations it was noted that the teachers tried various methods to manage their class which consisted of both typically developing children as well as children with special needs. While special attention was given to children with special needs, it was not always done as exclusively as in a special school due to manpower constraints and other limitations.

4.7 Recommended strategies from literature not utilized by participants

The use of PECS was one of the strategies recommended to be used for communication when dealing with children who have autism. But the participants did use picture cards but not in the proper way as recommended by Bondy and Frost (2001). The participants claimed that they did not use PECS because they were not trained formally to use PECS, nor did they have the resources supplied by the school. Even if picture cards were used, they were used at random without a proper system. Hence, teachers would benefit by being trained in the use of PECS so that this tool can be utilized to enhance communication with children with autism.

It was also recommended by Pressley and McCormick (1995) that whenever necessary, teachers could spend extra time after school hours to provide additional help to those children who need it. However, this was not observed among the participants who left their working place on time. One possible reason could be the long working hours faced by the teaching staff which prevents them from expending further time after their working hours to render further help to children who are slow in catching up with the rest of the class.

4.8 Level of acceptance in other typically developing children

P1 shared that when she went into the class, she would prepare the children for what to expect from the child with SEN and how to deal with it. She would tell them that he was special and different because he would exhibit certain behaviour which might seem unusual to them. For example, when the boy hugged his classmates, he might do so tightly and they would say, "Teacher, he is bullying us!" At that point, the teacher intervened and released his arms from behind him and showed him how to hug lightly. In this way, other typically developing children also learned how to handle such a situation without agitating him. This is supported by Diamond et al. (1997) who believe that having children with SEN in the same educational environment as other typically developing children promotes the teaching and learning of appropriate social behaviour for all. Through repetitive instructions, children learn to imitate proper behaviour from their peers and teachers (Bricker, 2000).

In addition, with the buddy system in place, P1 had observed that typically developing children had previously volunteered to be the buddy of a child with SEN. So, it was easier to assign a partner to that boy as the class generally had a positive perception of the child with SEN. This has been observed by Nabors (1997a) and Ervin et al. (1999) whereby children become more aware of their preferences for partnering. By providing an opportunity for typically developing children to partner their peers with SEN, there arises a situation whereby the differences among them are more acceptable by the children and they learn to adapt to the situation as well.

P2 mentioned that the other children were receptive to the special needs child's presence and were willing to share their toys with him. However, the teachers had to be vigilant at all times because that child had a tendency to be quick with his hands and might snatch something or hit someone when he got agitated. After the teachers explained to the whole class about his condition and what to expect from his behaviour, the children showed more understanding and less anxiety having him in their class. This understanding of their peer's condition leads to better acceptance and allows more interaction among the children (Diamond et al., 1997). In fact, when the teachers discussed the buddy system, the children had raised their hands to volunteer to be the boy's buddy. This indicates that the level of acceptance in other typically developing children was quite high in this class. Such demonstration of receptiveness of children with SEN has also been observed among typically developing children who have been exposed to children with SEN in a common learning environment (Peck et al., 1992).

In terms of acceptance, the participants felt that as these typically developing children were a bit older, with some of them having had attended the same preschool from playgroup age, and were more ready to help by partnering their classmates with SEN. With reminders from the teachers on how to deal with children who did not comprehend the teachers' instructions, these regular children were good at accepting these children as their friends and teammates. Hence, during playtime and mealtime, the child who had been assigned to guide the child with SEN sat next to him and told him what to do at that point. This was especially useful when they play games in pairs. At these times, the buddy system had been useful and it ensured that no one was left behind in whole class activities. This is in line with the findings of Ivory and McCollum (1999) who believed in the benefits of social play in developing children's language, social, cognitive and emotional development.

While there was some effort to encourage the rest of the children in the class to accept children with special needs through partnering and group work, there were some difficulties too. When a child had just had an outburst, then the child assigned to partner that child would show some reluctance in being his partner as there would be the fear that the child would hurt his partner again. At this point, the teacher would change his partner. If, at some point, it was not possible, then the teacher would personally become his partner for that activity until the children have forgotten the earlier temper tantrum episode and mingled around freely with that affected child. Thus, the teacher would have to use her discretion and see if the buddy system would work at that point. If it did not, then she would not force it, but modify it accordingly. Besides this, the teacher would also explain to the other children possible reasons as to why a particular child had an outburst earlier and alleviate any fear that the children might have about that child. Doing this constantly also helped the other children to be better prepared for any unpleasant situation that might arise and helped them to see it as an isolated incident and not to shun the child with the unruly behaviour totally. In this way, the teachers try to promote acceptance among the children.

As part of the teaching of appropriate behaviour, the teachers also include role-play. During these segments, the children would act out appropriate and inappropriate behaviour according to the teachers' instructions and elicit responses from the children as to which was good and which was bad behaviour. Through these role-play sessions, the children visually experience different types of scenarios which they would encounter in their own lives and share their responses with the rest of the class. This allowed the children to reflect upon their own behaviour and to correct their friends' behaviour if they found them to be inappropriate. Also, when the children re-enacted a certain scene, it brought the experience closer to their own experiences and helped in their understanding of the environment in which they live.

With the buddy system in place, the children were able to help one another in carrying out the tasks during each activity. At times when conflicts arose regarding sharing of materials, the teachers would use the picture cards to show the child "No snatching", "No shouting" and "Share". This had been quite helpful when used repeatedly as the child was able to visually comprehend what the teacher wanted him to do in that situation.

4.9 Views about additional support needs

The participants mentioned that there must be consistency among the teachers teaching a particular class in order to make their job more manageable. If a teacher had done things a certain way, then when another teacher comes along to take over the class at times, she should also follow the way the first teacher had done things. By doing so, the children would also not get confused and would be able to abide by the rules and follow the teacher's instructions clearly.

In terms of support from the parents of typically developing children, the participants mentioned that since these parents enrolled their children in this preschool knowing that this centre admits children with SEN, they are aware of the situation and give their full support to the teachers. Regarding on-going training, P1 mentioned the CICP course she attended after she was assigned the ICCP Nursery class. This class taught some basic points about children with special needs. In terms of support, P2 felt that she would like to know how else she could help the child with SEN. She believed that there could be other strategies used by teachers elsewhere that they could be introduced to so that their teaching could be more effective. Although P2 was not sure if the teachers would be sent for courses in future, she felt that the course she had attended did make her better prepared to handle children with special needs. In this sense, the school management committee had done their part in giving their support for the upgrading of the competency of their teaching staff. However, it is necessary to develop a separate pedagogy for children with SEN (Davis & Florian, 2004; Lewis & Norwich, 2005). Rather than leaving teachers to discover their own strategies to manage children with SEN, it would be of great help if a separate system was available for teachers to better guide children with SEN without impeding the learning experience of typically developing children.

Asked about any support the participants would like to have to further enhance their teaching experience in the preschool, the participants felt that if there could be additional therapy sessions for the children with SEN, it would be helpful. They believed that these children with SEN needed some expert guidance in terms of managing their temper tantrums and learning difficulties. Given the limited knowledge of the teachers in these areas, the participants felt that if extra sessions could be held as enrichment for these children, it would benefit them in the long run. The participants explained that while the teachers at the preschool were doing what they could, certain professional knowledge would help these children with SEN as they would get separate attention regularly like once a week or fortnightly so that these children do not get frustrated with not being able to catch up with their classmates in completing certain tasks.

Generally, the participants felt that if the school can arrange for additional therapy sessions by an external organization for the children with SEN, it would benefit the children and it also would be a great help to the teachers as they too can learn some strategies in managing them. At the end of the last interview, the participants mentioned that the school would be having counselling sessions for the children with SEN in the near future. In addition to these therapy sessions, P5, P6 and P7 felt that if they could have 2 more teachers to manage their class of 18, it would be beneficial to the teachers and the children. Currently, they did face some difficulties when more than one child threw a tantrum during lessons. While the teachers take turns to attend to the children who needed to be calmed down, having extra teachers would certainly help because the class was big, the children were still young and they needed to be assured that the situation was under control. These comments can be linked to the findings by Kristensen (2002), whereby teachers in that study also had concerns with the ratio between teacher and students.

In terms of support from the school management committee, the teachers felt that the teachers were given the liberty to use materials which were ready-made and to improvise and make their own resources. The school management committee would support the teachers financially if they needed to purchase resource materials and any other stationery item they might need in preparing lessons. Hence, while they have the set of PECs materials, the teachers also make their own picture cards and laminate them for class use. These were pasted on boards with Velcro so that they could be reused. However, they are not professionally trained in using PECS. As a result, the efficiency of using these materials may be reduced and may not produce the desired outcome.

Asked about any course that they had attended over the past 2 months, the participants mentioned that they had not attended any course formally except for the in-house training by a colleague who shared how she had made her own resources and how they could be used in class. The teachers found that particularly useful and also said that it gave them ideas about creating their own resources in a cost-effective way.

From the time of the second interview till the third, the participants had not attended any course to upgrade their skills. However, they were introduced to some ideas to be used in classroom activities through monthly staff meetings and e-mail correspondence among the teaching staff. The teachers get the notes during the meetings and through e-mail attachments, read them and try to implement some ideas in their own teaching where possible.

The next chapter contains a summary of the salient points discussed in this study, the findings from literature which is cross-referenced with the data collected and also some recommendations for future research.

Chapter Five:

Discussion

5.1 Introduction

The purpose of this study was to explore and explain how teachers in a preschool manage children with special needs in their classrooms. As believed by Ainscow and Miles (2008), the role of teachers is pivotal in making policy decisions about education as they are in the foreground of the playing field of any learning environment. Hence, this study was inspired by a personal interest in exploring what happened in a preschool which had a maximum enrolment of 10 children with special needs. Specifically, I wanted to understand what the teachers did to manage children with special needs together with typically developing children in their classrooms.

This study was based on Blumer's (1969) symbolic interaction theory. This theory holds that people make sense of the world they live in by assigning meanings to symbols in their interactions with their environment and the people around them. Hence, by the term 'manage', this study hoped to find out how teachers reacted to the situation they were placed in, i.e. a preschool which has children with special needs in the same learning environment as other typically developing children.

In order to gather data for the study, 3 semi-structured interviews and 3 observations were utilized over a period of 6 months. All the 8 teachers teaching in the preschool under study were involved in the data-collection process. After gathering the raw data, Miles and

Huberman's (1994) framework was used to analyse the data through the steps of data display, data reduction and drawing and verifying conclusions. In this chapter, the findings of the study are presented according to the research questions.

5.2 Research Question 1
Teachers' general views about having children with special needs in their classes

The findings of the study indicate that out of the 8 teachers involved six of them expressed initial anxiety over handling children with SEN together with other typically developing children. This was mainly due to the fact that they did not have any special training in this area at the point of joining this centre as a teacher. There was a general lack of confidence among the six teachers as they were unsure about the kinds of special needs the children could be having and how to manage them. Inexperience in managing an inclusive educational setting and insufficient knowledge of that field had contributed to the teachers' sense of being unprepared for the situation they are placed in. As held by the symbolic interaction theory, the term 'managing', as used in this context, refers to the way teachers perceive and react to the situations they are placed in (Chalmers & O'Donogue, 2000).

This sense of inadequacy was also found in Sparling's (2002) study. In fact, there was a sense of fear when the teachers were faced with a child with SEN. They constantly relied on their assisting teacher for help in handling them. While this was the initial reaction to having children with SEN in their classes, this negative view changed when they were interviewed 2 months later. The teachers seemed more at ease with children with SEN as they were able to understand their condition better. Furthermore, those teachers who were more confident in dealing with these children were constantly by their side, taking turns with carrying out certain activities. This gave the teachers some relief and they were able to learn certain strategies from their colleagues. By the time the teachers were interviewed 2 months later, their views were more positive and they appeared more confident to deal with their given situation. Hence, it can be observed that familiarity with the given situation reduces fear and boosts the confidence level of the teachers in this case.

5.3 Research Question 2
Strategies implemented by the teacher in the classroom to accommodate children with special needs

The findings of the study indicate that one of the strategies already in place at the beginning of the data collection period was the 'buddy-system'. This involved pairing a more capable child with another who might need some 'hand-holding'. While this system helped all the children generally, it was particularly useful for those children with SEN. Due to the demands of handling the children, the teachers could not always attend to each child personally. Hence, the 'buddy-system' was useful when the children helped one another during the classroom activities. While it provided a platform for children to learn by imitating appropriate social behaviour (Bricker, 2000), it also cultivated friendship and empathy among the children as the children are given the responsibility of taking care of and/or assisting a partner. From a young age, when children interact with their peers who have some form of disability, they become more aware and more ready to render help when requested (Diamond et al., 1997). On the whole, the buddy system not only benefits the children with special needs but all children generally who are exposed to an inclusive learning environment (Peck et al., 1992)

Another strategy used was using picture cards to communicate with the children. This strategy was used for all the children. When the teachers wanted to conduct an activity with minimum disruption and noise, the picture cards were used. The children were shown the cards to indicate the transition to the next activity. Especially for children with SEN, using picture cards reduced anxiety and the children seemed calm as they knew what to anticipate next. It was found that the teachers did not attend any formal training in the use of picture cards known as the Picture Exchange Communication System (PECs). However, they had made their own picture cards to indicate the activities that took place as routine in their classes. While the use of PECs is strongly recommended for children with autism (Charlop-Christy et al., 2002; Mirenda, 2008); Tien, 2008), the lack of formal training has put the teachers in this study in a disadvantaged position in not being able to utilize this useful tool in maximizing the learning experience of the children with SEN. Although the teachers in this study had improvised the use of picture cards in promoting communication, it would be optimal if the teachers had undergone formal training in this area.

The teachers also used 'time away' and 'time-out' as a strategy to manage unacceptable behaviours such as shouting or hurting another child during class activities. When a child displayed unruly behaviour, he was taken away from his classmates to another corner and given time to release his emotions through silent reflection. At times, the teachers would gently ask him why he behaved in a certain way and to counsel him on what would be the appropriate behaviour. These strategies are especially useful in managing inappropriate social behaviour among children who already have some difficulties in building social relationships (Bagwell et al., 2001; Webster-Stratton, 2001).

5.4 Research Question 3
How teachers encourage the rest of the children in the class to accept children with special needs

The findings of the study indicate that one of the ways the teachers tried to get the class to accept children with SEN as their friends was to tell the children about the special needs the children might be having and the kind of behaviour that they might be prepared to see during class activities. Through this, the children were mentally prepared for any unforeseen circumstances.

The buddy system was also useful as the children get to be partnered with someone and given the opportunity to help a friend. In fact it was observed that when the children were assigned to be partners of children with SEN, they did not resist the idea but were receptive to taking on the role. This could be due to the briefing the teachers had with the children about the condition of the children with special needs. With prior information given to them, the children were less fearful of their peers with special needs.

The teachers were also mindful of the way activities were organized. By specifying the rules to be abided by in the classroom, the teachers were able to indicate to the children the boundaries for acceptable behaviour and the consequences of inappropriate behaviour (Lewis et al., 2000). Usually, activities involved small group involvement or paired activities. This was done to facilitate more interaction among the children and to learn social skills like turn-taking and making polite requests which the children learn by imitating their peers (Bricker, 2000; Diamond et al., 1997).

Generally, the level of acceptance of children with special needs among the children was high and there was a willingness to accept these children into the regular class activities by the typically developing children. This was because the children had been exposed to children with special needs at a young age and they had learnt to accept the differences among them and adapt to the demands of the situation better (Diamond et al., 1997; Nabors, 1997a; Ervin et al., 1999). Thus, this shows that the younger the children are, the higher their level of acceptance of their peers with differences.

5.5 Research Question 4
Support that teachers expect to get from the school management committee in order to manage children with special needs

The findings of the study indicate that the teachers would like to have additional courses on managing children with special needs. While these teachers have undergone a module that covered handling children with special needs, they would like to be regularly updated on the latest strategies teachers have been using in other countries in similar settings. They would like to refine their knowledge of the special needs of the children under their care so that they would be more confident to handle them on their own (Bannister et al., 1998). With better knowledge, the teachers would be able to make modifications to their lessons, teaching strategies as well as the class structure so that learning takes place optimally for all the children present.

One major concern of this study, as was also observed by Kristensen (2002) in her research, was to increase the teacher-student ratio. The teachers would like to have additional manpower for classes with more than one child with special needs. This was expressed because the participants felt that with an additional teacher they would be able to carry out more varied activities as the children with special needs could be attended by a teacher while the rest of the class could be managed by the remaining teachers without much disruption to the plan, especially due to unforeseen episodes of temper-tantrums by the children.

The concerns of the teachers in this study are similar to those expressed by Kristensen (2002) who felt that insufficient resources and information about the kinds of special needs of the children under their care affected their level of confidence in managing their students. While these are some of the support expected by teachers who participated in this study, Clough and Lindsay (1991) suggest funding and additional special needs para-professionals, like educational psychologists, as further support for teachers in an inclusive educational environment.

5.6 Implications of Findings

This study examined teachers' perceptions and the strategies used in their classes. Generally, there were more positive responses to having children with special needs in their classes. However, teachers felt a sense of apprehensiveness towards their situation. This was mainly due to the lack of training and a sense of being overwhelmed by the teacher-student ratio which they believed made the situation challenging. Hence, there was not much specialised guidance provided for children with SEN, except for some temporary measures to deal with temper tantrums. The findings of this study is consistent with literature whereby lack of training for teachers and insufficient support from the school management committee were found to be barriers to accommodating children with special needs in mainstream educational settings.

5.7 Limitations of the research

The limitation was the use of a single site to conduct my research. The other preschools that admitted children with special needs in their schools rejected my proposal to use their school for my study. As a result, I was left with only one school which gave me permission to carry out my research with their condition of remaining anonymous.

The main difficulty of this research mainly existed in the form of time constraint. There were some occasions when I went to the preschool to conduct my research but could not conduct the interview as planned because one or two of the participants were on leave. Then, I had to arrange other alternative slots to carry out the interview. This was not that easy because the preschool had preplanned activities which involved bringing the children out of school and other training events that took some of the teachers away from the child care centre. As a result of this limitation, at some points, the schedule became tight and data collection sessions were close to one another. Yet generally, the entire process was completed with the full cooperation of the participants.

5.8 Merits of research

This research is valuable for its timeliness and relevance to the context, preschool inclusion in Singapore. While much discussion has been going on about inclusive preschool education internationally, I believe that there is still room for greater awareness and education in this area for education professionals as well as the stake holders in the society. While research has shown the benefits of an inclusive education system on young children before they embark on their formal education journey, there is still a certain level of skepticism revolving around this notion, doubts about the feasibility and its effectiveness on the children. While these are issues worth probing, I strongly believe that with appropriate support and procedures in place, implementation of the inclusive preschool education system is possible and is worth the effort. Hence, this research describes the current situation in a particular preschool and believes that the gaps found in the study would be a good source for future research.

5.9 Shortcomings of research

One drawback of this research is the limited sample population. If more than one preschool had participated in the study, perhaps a wider pool of data would have been available for deeper analysis. Then, the conclusions would have been better substantiated. In addition, if the study had been carried out over a period of one year, it would have been possible to see the effects of the strategies employed on students on a long-term basis.

5.10 Limitations

More preschools which accepted children with special needs could have been involved in this study to have a wide range of data. Then, a comparative study of the phenomenon and consequently different perspectives and a deeper analysis would have been made possible. However, the schools contacted were reluctant to participate in this study for fear of generating adverse opinions about their centre. Hence, for logistical reasons, this preschool was used to conduct the study.

In addition, if the study had been carried out over a period of one year, the data would have provided a broader scope for an in-depth analysis as the time span would have been substantial enough to observe longer term changes in the participants' mindsets and their measures implemented.

5.11 Recommendations

In this study it was found that had the teachers been sent for some specific training in managing children with special needs prior to taking up their posting as teachers in the preschool, there could have been less uncertainty and worry on the part of the teachers. They would have been equipped with at least some of the necessary knowledge and the strategies in managing children with special needs in their classes. Although there was some level of insecurity on the part of the teachers when they had to manage children with special needs, over time, with the assistance of colleagues, the teachers' fears were alleviated and they felt more confident to deal with their situation. Hence, with pre-service training and in-service training, teachers could be considerably better prepared to deal with children with special needs in their classes.

In addition, with better knowledge of current trends in preschool education, especially ones that include children with special needs to attend school alongside typically developing children, teachers would be better able to adapt the current curriculum and teaching materials according to the needs of their classes.

When educators are able to track their own attitudes, work with others in collaboration and make changes to their own curriculum and teaching strategies by learning from other teachers, it benefits all children. In fact, one of the participants of this study mentioned that teacher-training programmes should include segments on strategies for teaching and behaviour management aspects. In view of this comment, it is important that teachers not only be competent in developing a sound curriculum but also have the expertise to modify current practices according to the needs of the setting they are in. Such a curriculum would be beneficial to both the children in the preschool as well as the teachers who would be managing a diverse group of children in their classes.

In order for the management to upgrade the skills of the teaching staff and acquire latest materials for the teachers to use in class, there has to be more open communication and clear expression of the current situation in actual classroom settings. If the teachers could raise their concerns frankly to the school management committee, then necessary changes could me made to cater to the growing needs of the children and the teachers. Hence, there should be open channels of communication and receptiveness on the part of both the teachers and the school management committee.

The teachers stated that they were apprehensive when they were initially told that there would be children with special needs in their classes. Based on the results of this study, the researcher recommends that all teachers be sent for training before they take over a class which has children with special needs regardless of the number of years of experience. In addition to this initial training, teachers should also be sent for yearly courses to upgrade their knowledge and skills in this area. This is to facilitate professional growth of the teachers to keep abreast with changing trends in education.

Further studies that compare the level of competencies of teachers before they attended courses on managing children with special needs and after they had attended, are needed to see the effect training has on the level of confidence of teachers on dealing with children with special needs could be carried out to track the impact of the training on the level of competency of the teachers. While this may lead to overloading the teachers who may have to attend other courses pertaining to curriculum, pedagogy, management and others, perhaps staggering these courses over a period of time might help.

Teachers do not have the necessary materials to teach children with special needs. The current materials they are using are those that are used for typically developing children and those that are prepared by the teachers themselves. To ensure that the children with special needs are getting the right teaching materials appropriate to their level of needs, the school should purchase professionally produced materials. Furthermore, teachers should be sent for training on how to use the materials they have acquired so that the children under their care benefit from their usage.

Teachers have limited knowledge about children with special needs and rely on their co-teachers to help when there is a crisis. These co-teachers are not teachers who have taught in a special school. Thus, the researcher recommends that a special needs officer (SNO) be employed in this preschool to give expert advice and assistance for the teachers. With the presence of the SNO, the teachers would be more confident in dealing with the situation knowing well that at any point of emergency, the SNO can be called upon. This would reduce their anxiety and make them mentally calm enough to attend to delivering their lessons to the children.

Teachers felt that there should be more open communication between the school management staff and the teachers. Due to limited time especially, there is not enough conversation between these two bodies. Hence, the researcher recommends that certain communication modes be made available for the teachers, such as more group discussion between the various class teachers and the management committee so that teachers can express their current concerns and the management committee can also share their limitations and expectations of the teachers. Such an open communication would bring the two groups closer to each other and their thoughts can be aligned to benefit the children in their preschool.

Another recommendation for future research would be including the parents of children with special needs and typically developing children in the study. It would be interesting to find out how the parents view the whole situation and how well they welcome it. In this way, we would be able to obtain a more holistic view of the inclusive education scene in Singapore.

References

Ahuja, A. (2005). *EFA National Action Plans Review Study: Key Findings.* Bangkok, UNESCO.

Ainscow, M., Beresford, J., Harris, A., Hopkins, D., Southworth, G. & West, M. (2000) *Creating the Conditions for School Improvement.* 2nd Ed. London: David Fulton Publishers.

Ainscow, M. (2005). Developing inclusive education systems: what are the levers for change? *Journal of Educational Change* 6, pp 109-124

Ainscow, M., Dyson, A., Booth, T. Dyson, A. (2006). Improving schools, developing inclusion. London: Routledge (Taylor & Francis)

Ainscow, M., & Miles, S. (2008), Making education for all inclusive, *PROSPECTS*, pp 15-34.

Alper, S., & Ryndak, D. L. (1992). Educating students with severe handicaps in regular classes. *The Elementary School Journal,* pp 373-387.

American Academy of Pediatrics. (2001). Clinical practice guideline: Treatment of the school-aged child with attention-deficit/hyperactivity disorder. *Pediatrics,* pp 1033-1044.

Armstrong, T. (1996). A holistic approach to attention deficit disorder. *Education Leadership,* pp 34-36.

August, G.J., Realmuto G.M., Hektner, J.M., & Bloomquist, M.L. (2001). An intergrated components preventive intervention for aggressive elementary school children: *The Early Risers Program. Journal of Consulting and Clinical Psychology,* pp 614-626.

Bagwell, C.L., Molina, B.S., Pelham, Jr., W.E., & Hoza, B. (2001). Attention-deficit hyperactivity disorder and problems in peer relations: Predictions from childhood to adolescence. *Journal of the American Academy of Child and Adolescent Psychiatry,* pp 1285-1292.

Banerji, M. & Dailey, R. (1995). A Study of the Effectiveness of an Inclusion Model on Students with Specific Learning Disabilities. *Journal of Learning Disabilities,* pp 511-522.

Bannister, C., Sharland, V., Thomas, G., Upton, V. & Walker, D. (1998) Changing from a special school to an inclusion service. *British Journal of Special Education,* pp 65-69.

Barkley, R. A. (1998). *Attention-deficit hyperactivity disorder: a handbook for diagnosis and treatment.* New York: Guilford Press.

Barkley, R. A., Fischer, M., Smallish, L., & Fletcher, K. (2002). The persistence of attention deficit/hyperactivity disorder into young adulthood as a function of reporting source and definition of disorder. *Journal of Abnormal Psychology,* pp 279-289.

Bereiter, C. & Engelman, S. (1966). Teaching disadvantaged children in the preschool. Engelwood Cliffs, NJ: Prentice-Hall.

Berg, B.L. (2004) *Qualitative research methods.* 5th Ed. California State University: Pearson.

Bloh, C. & Axelrod, A. (2009). "Behavior Should Be Enough: Growing Support for Using Applied. Behavior Analysis in the Classroom. *Journal of Early Behaviour Intervention,* 5(2), pp 52-56.

Blumer, H. (1969). *Symbolic interactionism; perspective and method.* Englewood Cliffs, N.J.: Prentice-Hall.

Bondy, A.S. (2001). PECS: Potential Benefits and Risks. *The Behaviour Analyst Today,* 2, pp 127-132.

Bondy, A.S. and Frost, L. (2001). *A Picture's Worth: PECS and Other Visual Communication Strategies in Autism (Topics in Autism),* UK: Woodbine House.

Booth, T. and Ainscow, M. (2000). *Index on Inclusion.* Bristol: Centre for Studies on Inclusive Education.

Bricker, D. (2000). Inclusion: How the Scene has Changed. *Topics in Early Childhood Special Education,* pp 14-19.

Brown, W., Odom, S, Shouming Li, & Zercher, C. (1999). Ecobehavioral Assessment in Early Childhood Programs: A Portrait of Preschool Inclusion. *Journal of Special Education,* pp 138-153.

Buysse, V., Goldman, B.D., & Skinner, M. L. (2002). Setting effects on friendship formation among young children with and without disabilities. Exceptional Children, pp 503-517.

Carpenter, L. & Emerald, E. (2009). Stories from the margin: Mothering a child with ADHD or ASD. Teneriffe, Queensland: Post Pressed.

Chalmers, R & O'Donoghue, T. (2000). How teachers manage their work in inclusive classrooms. *Teaching and Teacher Education*, pp 889-904.

Charlop-Christy, M.H., et al. (2002). Using the Picture Exchange Communication System (PECS) With Children With Autism: Assessment of PECS Acquisition, Speech, Social-Communicative Behaviour, and Problem Behaviour. *Journal of Applied Behaviour Analysis*, pp 213-231.

Chen, K. and Tan, S. Y. (2006) "Education and services for children and youth with emotional/behavioral problems in Singapore", *Preventing School Failure*, pp 37-42.

Chenitz, W.C. & Swanson, J.M. (1986). *From practice to grounded theory: Qualitative research in nursing.* California: Addison-Wesley.

Clough, P. & Lindsay, G. (1991) Integration and the support service. Changing roles in special education. London: Routledge Falmer

Coates, R.D. (1989) The regular Education Initiative and opinions of regular classroom teachers, *Journal of Learning Disabilities*, pp 532-536

Code of Ethics. *The Living Document: Guidelines for professional responsibilities in early childhood education. AECES (Association For Early Childhood Educators (Singapore))*

Cohen, H., Amerine-Dickens, M., & Smith, T. (2006). Early intensive behavioral treatment: Replication of the UCLA Model in a community setting. *Journal of Developmental and Behavioral Pediatrics*, pp 145-155

Corbett, J. (2001). *Supporting Inclusive Education. A Connective Pedagogy.* New York: Routledge Falmer.

Cook, B. (2001). A Comparison of Teachers' Attitudes Towards Their Included Students With Mild and Severe Disabilities. *The Journal of Special Education,* pp 203-213.

Costenbader, A. (2000). A Comparison of Developmental Gains for Preschool Children with Disabilities in Inclusive and Self-Contained Classrooms. *Topics in Early Childhood Special Education*, pp 224-235.

Darling-Hammond, L. (May 2003). Keeping good teachers; Why it matters, what leaders can do. *Educational Leadership*, pp 6-13.

Davis, P. & Florian, L. (2004). *Journal of Teaching strategies and approaches for pupils with special educational needs: a scoping study.* DfES Publications.

Diamond, K., Hestenes, L., Carpenter, E. & Innes, F. (1997) Relationships Between Enrollment in an Inclusive Class and Preschool Children's Ideas about People with Disabilities. *Topics in Early Childhood Special Education*, pp 520-536.

Dinnebeil, L. A., McInerney, W., Fox, C., & Juchartz-Pendry, K. (1998). An analysis of the perceptions and characteristics of childcare personnel regarding inclusion of young children with special needs in community-based programs. *Topics in Early Childhood Special Education, pp* 188-128.

Doyle, W. (1986). Classroom organization and management. In Merlin C. Wittrock (Ed.) *Handbook of Research on Teaching, 4th Edition.* New York: MacMillan Publishing.

Duhaney, D. C. (2004). Blended learning in education, training, and development. *Performance Improvement,* pp 35-38.

Dyson, A. and Millward A. (2000). *Schools and special needs: Issues of innovation and inclusion.* London: Paul Chapman.

Early Childhood Research Institute on Inclusion (2000). *Retrieved on 1 November 2011 from www.fpg.unc.edu/~ecrii/.*

Erwin, E., Alimaras, E. & Price, N. (1999). A Qualitative Study of the Social Dynamics in an Inclusive Preschool. *Journal of Research in Childhood Education*, pp 56-67.

Feagin, J.R., Orum, A.M. & Sjoberg, G. (1991). *A Case for the Case Study Book.* University of North Carolina Press. Chapel Hill, NC.

Firestone, W.A (2003). *Alternative Arguments for Generalizing From Data as Applied to Qualitative Research.* Educational Researcher. Michigan: American Educational Research Association.

Frederickson, N. & Cline, T. (2009) *Special Educational Needs, Inclusion and Diversity: A Textbook.* 2nd Ed. Buckingham : Open University Press.

Freire, S. & César, M. (2002). Evolution of the Portuguese education system. A deaf child's life in a regular school: Is it possible to have hope? *Educational and Child Psychology,* pp 76-96.

Fung, D. & Lee, T.S. (2009) Attention Deficit Hyperactivity Disorder: coping or curing? *Annals of the Academy of Medicine, Singapore,* pp 916-7.

Gall, M.D., Gall, J.P., & Borg, W.R. (2003). *Educational research: An introduction.* 7th Ed. Boston: Allyn & Bacon.

Garrett, J.N. & Kelley, M. (2000). Early Childhood Special Education. *Association for Childhood Education International.* Retrieved November 2, 2011 from High Beam Research: http://www.highbeam.com/doc/1G1-63089238.html

Garfinkle, A.N., & Schwartz, I.S. (1996). Observational learning in an integrated preschool: Effects on peer imitation and social interaction. Unpublished manuscript, University of Washington.

Gibson, M. (2005). *Opportunities and Challenges: Additional Support for Learning (Scotland) Act 2004.* Paper delivered at a conference in Dublin by Mike Gibson, the Head of the Additional Support Needs Division in the Education Department of the Scottish Executive.

Guralnick, M. J. (2005). Early intervention for children with intellectual disabilities: Current knowledge and future prospects. *Journal of Applied Research in Intellectual Disabilities,* pp 313-324.

Hains, A.H., Fowler, S. A., Schwartz, I. S., Kottwitz, E., & Rosenkoetter, S. (1989). A comparison of preschool and kindergarten expectations for school readiness. *Early Childhood Research Quarterly,* pp 75-88.

Halasz, G. (2002). 'Smartening up or dumbing down?: A look behind the symptoms, overprescribing and reconceptualizing ADHD', in G. Halasz, G. Anaf, P. Ellingsen, A. Manne & F. Thomson Salo, *Cries unheard: A new look at attention deficit hyperactivity disorder,* pp 75-91. Altona, VIC: Common Ground

Hargreaves, L. (2009) 'The status and prestige of teachers and teaching', in Saha, L. and Dworkin, G. (Eds.) *The Springer International Handbook of Research on Teachers and teaching (Vol 21. Part 1)* (pp 217-230). New York: Springer.

Harris, S.L.P., & Delmolino, L.P. (2002). Applied Behaviour Analysis: Its Application in the Treatment of Autism and Related Disorders in Young Children. *Infants and Young Children*, pp 11-17.

Hinshaw, S. (2002). Is ADHD an Impairing Condition in Childhood and Adolescence?. *In* P.S.Jensen & J.R.Cooper (Eds.), *Attention deficit hyperactivity disorder: State of the science, best practices*, pp 5-21. Kingston, New Jersey. Civic Research Institute.

Houk, G.M., King, M.C., Tomlinson, B., Vrabel, A., & Wecks, K. (2002). Small group intervention for children with attention disorders. *Journal of School Nursing*, pp 196-200.

Howard, J.S., et al. (2005). A Comparison of Intensive Behaviour Analytic and Eclectic Treatments for Young Children with Autism. *Research on Developmental Disability*, pp 359-383.

Hundert, J., Mahoney, B., Mundy, F., & Vernon, M. L. (1998). A descriptive analysis of developmental and social gains of children with severe disabilities in segregated and inclusive preschools in southern Ontario. *Early Childhood Research Quarterly*, pp 49-65.

Hyde, K.L., Samson, F., Evans, A.E & Mottron, L. (2010). Neuroanatomical differences in brain areas implicated in perceptual and other core features of autism revealed by cortical thickness analysis and voxel-based morphometry. *Human Brain Mapping*, pp 556-66.

Ivory, J. & McCollum, J. (1999). Effects of Social and Isolate Toys on Social Play in an Inclusive Setting. *The Journal of Special Education*, pp 238-243.

Jensen, V.K., & Sinclair, L.V. (2002). Treatment of Autism in Young Children: Behavioural Intervention and Applied Behaviour Analysis. *Infants and Young Children*, pp 42-52.

Kanu, S. A. (2008). Special Needs Education in Perspective. In A. Olabisi (ed.) *Child Care and Special Needs Education in Nigeria.* Jos: Centre for Learning Disabilities and audiology, pp 1-12.

Korpan, C.A., Bisanz, J., Boehme, C., & Lynch, M.A. (1997). What did you learn outside of school today? Using structured interviews to document home and community activities related to science and technology. *Science Education*, pp 651-662.

Kristensen, K. (2002). *Proposals for Adjustment of Education of Learners with Barriers to Learning and Development into Ordinary School Settings.* Ministry of Education and Sport, Kampala, Uganda.

Kristensen, K., Omagor-Loican, M., Onen, N., & Okot, D. (2006). *Opportunities for inclusion? The education of learners with special educational needs and disabilities in special schools in Uganda.* British journal of special education, pp 139-147.

Ladson-Billings, G. (1994). *The Dreamkeepers: Successful teaching for African-American students.* San Francisco: Jossey-Bass, pp 17-18.

Lamorey, S., & Bricker, D. D. (1993). Integrated programs: Effects on young children and their parents. In C. Peck, S. Odom, & D. Bricker (Eds.), *Integrating young children with disabilities into community-based programs: From research to implementation,* pp 249-269. Baltimore: Brookes.

LaRossa, R. and Reitzes, D.C. (1993) Symbolic interactionism and family studies. In P. G. Boss, W. J. Doherty, R. LaRossa, W. R. Schumm, & S. K. Steinmetz (Eds.), *Sourcebook of family theories and methods: A contextual approach,* pp 135-163. New York: Plenum Press.

LeRoy, B. & Simpson, C. (1996) Improving student outcomes through inclusive education, *Support for Learning,* pp 32-36.

Lewis, A. & Norwich, B. (Eds.) (2005). *Special teaching for special children? Pedagogies for inclusion.* Buckingham: Open University Press.

Lewis, T. Sugai, G. & Colvin, G. (2000). Reducing problem behaviour through a school-wide system of effective behavioral support: Investigation of a school-wide social skills training program and contextual interventions. *School Psychology Review,* pp 446-459.

Lian, W.B., Ho, S.K., Yeo, C.L. & Ho, L.Y. (2003). General practitioners' knowledge on childhood developmental and behavioural disorders. *Singapore Medical Journal,* pp 397-403.

Lian, W.B., Ying, S.H., Tean, S.C., Lin, D.C., Lian, Y.C.& Yun, H.L. (2008). Pre-school teachers' knowledge, attitudes and practices on childhood developmental and behavioural disorders in Singapore. *Journal of Paediatric Child Health*, pp 187-94.

Lovaas, O. (1987). Behavioural Treatment and Normal Educational and Intellectual Functioning in Young Autistic Children. *Journal of Consultative Clinical Psychology*, pp 3-9.

Mastropieri, M.A., Scruggs, T.E., Graetz, J., Fontana, Coles, V., & Gerson, A. (2004). Mnemonic strategies: What are they? How can I use them? And how effective are they? In M. K. Riley & T. A. Citro (Eds). *Best practices for all children in the inclusionary classroom: Leading researchers talk directly with teachers* (pp 49-64). Boston: Massachusetts Learning Disabilities Association.

MCYS (2009).*Guide to Setting Up A Child care Centre*, ww.childcarelink.gov.sg

Miles, M.B. & Huberman, A.M. (1994). An Expanded Sourcebook, Qualitative Data Analysis (2ⁿᵈ Ed.), California and London: Sage Publications. Inc.

Ministry of Education, Singapore. MOE Press Releases. (2010). *MOE to Provide Greater Support for Special Education*. Retrieved from MOE website on 1 November, 2011.

Mirenda, P. (2008). A back door approach to autism and AAC. *Augmentative and Alternative Communication*, pp 219-233.

Mulryan, C. (1995). Fifth and sixth graders' involvement and participation in cooperative small groups in mathematics. *The Elementary School Journal.* pp 297-310.

Nabors, L. (1997a). Playmate Preferences of Children Who are Typically Developing for their Classmates with Special Needs. *Mental Retardation*, pp 107-13.

Nabors, L. (1997b). Social interaction among preschool children in inclusive child care centers. *Applied Developmental Science*, pp 162-167.

Nelson, J., Johnson, A. & Marchand-Martella, N. (1996). Effects of direct instruction, cooperative learning, and independent learning practices on the classroom behavior of students with behavioral disorders: A comparative analysis. *Journal of Emotional and Behavioral Disorders,* pp 53-62.

Nomanbhoy, D. M., Lim, L., & Vasudev, R. (2000). Promoting quality care and education for preschoolers with disabilities in mainstream settings: The TEACHME services. In C. Tan-Niam & M. L. Quah (Eds.), *Investing in our future: The early years* (pp. 200-211). Singapore: McGraw-Hill.

Noonan, M. J., & McCormick, L. (1993). *Early intervention in natural settings.* Pacific Grove, CA: Brooks/Cole.r future

Nunan, D. (1992). *Research methods in language learning.* Cambridge: Cambridge University Press.: The

O'Brien, T. (Ed.). (2001). *Enabling Inclusion: Blue Skies . . . Dark Clouds?* London: The Stationery Office. future: The early years (pp. 200-211).

Odom, S. (2000). Preschool Inclusion: What We Know and Where We Go From Here. *Topics in Early Childhood Special Education,* pp 20-27.

Ospina, M. B., Krebs Seida, J., Clark, B., Karkhaneh, M., Hartling, L., Tjosvold, L., Vandermeer, B. & Smith, V. (2008). *Behavioural and developmental interventions for autism spectrum disorder: a clinical systematic review.* Alberta Research Centre for Health Evidence, University of Alberta, Edmonton, Alberta, Canada.

Peck, C. A., Carlson, P. & Helmstetter, E. (1992). Parent and teacher perceptions of outcomes for typically developing children enrolled in integrated early childhood programs: A statewide survey. *Journal of Early Intervention,* pp 53-63.

Polanczyk, G. de Lima M.S., Horta B.L., Biederman, J. & Rohde, L.A. (2007). The worldwide prevalence of ADHD: a systematic review and metaregression analysis. *Journal of Psychiatry,* pp 942-8.

Poon-McBrayer, K., & Lian, M-G.J. (2002). *Special Needs Education: Children with Exceptionalities.* Hong Kong: The Chinese University Press.

Poon, K.K., Conway, R.N., & Khaw, J., (2007). An Ecological Framework for Understanding and Intervention Planning of Students with Special Needs. In *Supporting Students with Special Needs in Mainstream Schools.* Singapore: Prentice Hall, Pearson Education South Asia, pp 19-41.

Porter, L. (2002). *Educating young children with additional needs.* Australia: Allen & Unwin.

Pressley, M., & Mc Cormick, C. (1995). *Advanced Educational Psychology.* New York: Harper Collins.

Punch, K.F. (2005). *Introduction to Social Research-Quantitative & Qualitative Approaches.* 2nd Ed. London: Sage.

Quah, M. M., Lim, L., & Poon-McBrayer, K. F. (2004). *Special Education in Singapore: Celebrating the past, envisioning the future.* Association for Supervision and Curriculum Development (Singapore)

Renard, L. (2003). Setting new teachers up for failure or success. *Educational Leadership,* pp 62-64.

Retas, S. & Kwan, C. (2000). Preschool Quality and Staff Characteristics in Singapore. In C. Tan-Niam &. M. L. Quah (Eds). *Investing in our Future: the early years.* Singapore: McGraw-Hill.

Rosenwasser, B., & Axelrod, S. (2001). The Contribution of Applied Behaviour Analysis to the Education of People with Autism: *Behaviour Modification,* pp 671-677.

Sakarneh, M. (2008). Effective Teaching in Inclusive Classroom: Literature Review. AARE International Education Research Conference, Melbourne. http://ww.aare.edu.au/04pap/

Schwartz, I.S., et al. (1998). The Picture Exchange Communication System: Communicative Outcomes for Young Children with Disabilities. *Topics in Early Childhood Special Education,* pp 144-159.

Semmel, M.I., Abernathy, T.V., Butera, G. & Lesar, S. (1991). Teacher perceptions of the Regular Education Initiative, *Exceptional Children,* pp 9-24.

Simpson, R.L. (2001a). Early Intervention with Children with Autism: The Search for Best Practices. *Journal of the Association for Persons with Severe Handicaps,* pp 218-221.

Simpson, R.L. (2001b). ABA and Students with Autism Spectrum Disorders: Issues and Considerations for Effective Practice. *Focus on Autism and Other Developmental Disabilities*, pp 68-71.

Sparling, E. (2002). Social acceptance at senior high school. *International Journal of Special Education*, pp 91-100

Stake, R. (1995). *The art of case study research.* Thousand Oaks, CA: Sage Publications.

Stiefel, I., Shields, A., Swain, M. & Innes, W. (2008). 'Asperger's coming out of our ears: Making sense of a modern epidemic', *Australian and New Zealand Journal of Family Therapy*, pp 1-9.

Stright, A. & Supplee, L. (2002). Children's self-regulatory behaviors during teacher-directed, seat-work, and small-group instructional contexts. *The Journal of Educational Research, 95*(4).

Tien, K. (2008). Effectiveness of the Picture Exchange Communication System as a Functional Communication Intervention for individuals with Autism Spectrum Disorders: A Practice-Based Research Synthesis. *Education and Training in Developmental Disabilities*, pp 61-76.

Trochim, W. (2000). *The Research Methods Knowledge Base*, 2nd Edition. Cincinnati, OH: Atomic Dog Publishing.

UNESCO Policy Brief on Early Childhood (2007), *Partnership with Non-Public Actors: Singapore's Early Childhood Policy*, www.unesco. org/education/earlychildhood/brief

UNICEF (May 2008), *Division of Policy and Practice, Statistics and Monitoring Section*, www.childinfo.org

United Nations Educational, Scientific and Cultural Organization (UNESCO) (1994). *The Salamanca Statement and Framework for Action on Special Needs Education*, Paris, UNESCO.

United Nations World Summit Outcome (2005). www.un.org/summit2005/presskit/fact_sheet.pdf

U.S. Department of Health and Human Services (1999). Mental Health: A Report of the Surgeon General-Executive Summary. U.S. Department of Health and Human Services, Substance Abuse and Mental Health Services Administration, Center for Mental Health

Services, National Institutes of Health. National Institute of Mental Health, Rockville, MD.

Vaughn, S., Schumm, J.S., Jallad, B., Slusher, J. & Saumell, L. (1996) Teachers' views of inclusion, *Learning Disabilities Research and Practice*, pp 96-106

Verschuren, P. J. M. (2003). Case study as a research strategy: Some ambiguities and opportunities. *International Journal of Social Research Methodology*, pp 121-139.

Villa, R.A., Thousand, J.S., Meyers, H. & Nevin, A. (1996) Teacher and administrator perceptions of heterogeneous education, *Exceptional children*, pp 29-45.

Walker, H.M., Colvin, G., & Ramsey, E. (1995). *Antisocial behaviour in school: Strategies and best practices*. Pacific Grove, CA: Brooks/Cole Publishing Company.

Walker, H., Horner, R., Sugai, G., Bullis, M., Sprague, J., Bricker, D. & Kaufman, M. (1996). Integrated approaches to preventing antisocial behavior patterns among school-age children and youth. *Journal of Emotional and Behavioral Disorders,* pp 194-209.

Webster-Stratton, C., Reid, M.J., & Hammond, M. (2001). Social skills and problem solving training for children with early-onset conduct problems: who benefits? *Journal of Child Psychology and Psychiatry*, pp 943-952.

Whitten. E. & Campos, L. (2003). Annual Editions: Educating Exceptional Children. *Retrieved on 1 November, 2011 from www. essaythesis.net/2011/04/early-childhood-special-education.html.*

Wilkins-Canter, E. A., Edwards, E., Young, A., Ramanathan, H., & McDougle, K. (2000). Preparing novice teachers to handle stress. *Kappa Delta Pi Record*, pp 128-130.

Wilmore, E.L. (1995). When your child is special. *Educational Leadership*, pp 60-62.

Wing. L. & Gould, J. (1979). Severe impairments of social interaction and associated abnormalities in children: epidemiology and classification. *Journal of Autism Developmental Disorder.* pp 11-29.

Wolfberg, P.J. & Schuler, A.L. (1999). Fostering peer interaction, imaginative play and spontaneous *language in children with autism, Child Language Teaching and Therapy Journal.* pp 41-52.

Woo, B.S.C., Ng. T.P., Fung, D.S.S., Chan, Y.H., Lee, Y.P., Koh, J.B.K., (2007).
Emotional and behavioural problems in Singaporean children based on parent, teacher and child reports. *Singapore Medical Journal,* pp 1100-6.

*World Vision (2007). I*ncluding the excluded. Integrating disability into the EFA Fast Track Initiative processes and National Education Plans in Cambodia. *www.worldvision.org.uk/what-we-do/advocacy/ . . . / research-reports/*

Yamaguchi, K. (2005). Development of Special Needs Education in Japan and Some Current Problems. *Inclusive and Supportive Education Congress*
International Special Education Conference. Inclusion: Celebrating Diversity? Glasgow, Scotland.

Yin, Robert K. (2003). *Case Study Research: Design and Methods.* London: Sage Publications.

References from Websites

www.aeces.org/code_of_ethics/2011
www.autism.org.sg/2011
www.learningtrust.co.uk/special_needs/what_schools_do/iep.aspx/ 2012
www.mcys.gov.sg/2011
www.metta.org.sg/english/abt_media_archive.html/2011
www.moe.gov.sg/education/preschool/teachers/2011
www.moe.gov.sg/1995
www.moe.gov.sg/2002
www.moe.gov.sg/2004
www.moe.gov.sg/2008
www.moe.gov.sg/2011
www.ncss.gov.sg/social_service/enabling_masterplan.asp/2012
www.schoolbag.sg, March/ 2010
www.singapore21.org.sg

Appendix One

Guiding questions for 1ˢᵗ interview:

1. Generally, what do you feel about teaching children with special needs?

   _____

   _____

   _____

   _____

   _____

2. What strategies do you use to accommodate children with special needs in mainstream classes? How does this happen on a daily basis?

   _____

   _____

   _____

   _____

   _____

3. How do you encourage the rest of the children in the class to accept children with special needs?

   _____

   _____

   _____

   _____

   _____

4. What kind of support do you expect to get from the school management committee to allow the inclusion of children with special needs to take place?

_____

_____

_____

_____

_____

Appendix Two

Guiding questions for 2ⁿᵈ interview:

1. From the beginning of the year till now, how have your general believes about teaching children with special needs changed? In terms of your ability to manage these children, how do you feel over the past few months?

   _____

   _____

   _____

   _____

   _____

2. Could you please elaborate on some of the educational strategies implemented in your classroom so far this year to accommodate children with special needs? What are some of the problems you encountered in doing so?

   _____

   _____

   _____

   _____

   _____

3. Could you give some examples to show how you encourage the rest of the children in the class to accept children with special needs? Were there some difficulties? Please explain.

_____

_____

_____

_____

_____

4. In what ways has the school management committee been helpful to teachers in allowing the inclusion of children with special needs to take place? Have you used any new materials/ attended courses etc. to learn more about teaching children with special needs in mainstream learning environment?

_____

_____

_____

_____

_____

Appendix Three

Guiding questions for 3rd interview:

1. Over the past six months, have your general thoughts and feelings about teaching children with special needs changed? If so, please explain how. What can you say about your ability to manage these children during this period of time?

   _____

   _____

   _____

   _____

   _____

2. Have you adapted or implemented any strategies to assist in the learning of children with special needs? Please explain.

   _____

   _____

   _____

   _____

   _____

3. From the beginning of the year till now, what have you observed about the level of acceptance in your class regarding children with special needs?

_____

_____

_____

_____

_____

4. For the past six months, what kind of assistance is provided by the school management committee to make it easier for teachers to manage an inclusive classroom?

_____

_____

_____

_____

_____